ANCIENT MYSTERIES OF HEALING DISCOVERED

ॐ

ANCIENT MYSTERIES OF HEALING DISCOVERED

℘

Tom Milliren

Edited by Karen Troiani

ANGEL 99

This text should not be considered an exclusing method of confronting medical problems. It should be viewed as an adjunct to orthodox medical or psychological treatment, unless contrary medical advise is given.

Published by: Angel 99
RD#1, Box 180A-1
New Florence, PA 15944

Edited: Karen Troiani
Cover design & graphics: Leslie Carrere
Illustrations: Bill Benson
Printed in the United States of America
Photo of Tom Milliren by Village Photography
Photo of Karen Troiani by Park Cover

Printed in the USA by

*M*ORRIS
PUBLISHING

3212 E. Hwy 30
Kearney, NE 68847
800-650-7888

Contents

ANCIENT MYSTERIES OF HEALING DISCOVERED

Foreword

I made a covenant with Spirit and my spirit guides a number of years ago that I would dedicate myself to helping people find their reality and to know they are of the intelligence called God. The information presented in this book is directed toward describing and explaining the nature and principles associated with human energy systems and interdimensional communication. It also provides basic instruction for several very successful methods of healing.

The extent to which you can accept and prepare yourself to use the information will be a very personal experience. The information has been received through the highest spiritual order of our source intelligence, the God spirit, and through the light and teachings of spirit guides. Therefore it is protected against those who would use the information against others as an act of greed, ego or service to self as a primary intent.

The process of communication between conscious, sub-conscious, and super-conscious parts of the mind and the teachings of enlightened messengers from Spirit is through a phenomenon called dowsing. This medium of intellectual communication beyond the physical dimension has been known and used since ancient times. Through this medium we are able to safely make contact with the vibrational dimensions comprising the unseen energy that presents a new and expanded experience of our own human reality. The dynamics of this research prove itself by the fact that these methods produce positive effects in the human organism.

Editor's Introduction

Recently, the idea that health and healing stretch beyond allopathic medicine has become a common one. Beyond the limits of the physical body there are factors which are intelligent and affect the body both positively and negatively. This area of study is difficult to define in present day science and technology as the aura is an intangible thing. However, through dowsing, Tom has successfully mapped the aura energy field and by comparing hundreds and hundreds of case studies, has been able to post some markers for the conscious mind to address the ephemeral.

The benefits of being able to dowse the aura to pinpoint anomalies for correction is significant for the conscious mind of the facilitator as well as the client. The client can watch the dowsing rod or pendulum as it reacts indicating the location of the aura energy field as well as holes or depressions located in the field. Although the interpretation of the dowsing instrument is potentially different for each dowser, there is a physical item to look at. For some clients, this is easier to accept than a mysterious psychic evaluation (although not necessarily more or less accurate). Confidence is gained as the novice learns to interpret the dowsing instrument and to trust his/her own interpretation.

Working with Tom has been an incredible experience. I have watched him measure countless auras, perform spirit clearings and regressions with equal caring and compassion. His ability to remain completely engrossed and focused on the person at hand is incomparable. This departure from ego involving personal gain or profit has no doubt affected his success rate in a positive light to an amazing 98% in dowsing for water with an equally high success rating for effecting positive personal change in persons with physical, mental and emotional anomalies.

In an effort to shed some light on the ephemeral aura, this book is intended for those striving to help others. Naturally, through the process, we benefit ourselves as well. The guidelines presented here are an effort to improve the human condition through work with Spirit for the highest and best good of all. Occasionally, even in trying to do good, without proper instruction from a qualified healer, psychic difficulties can arise. How do you find a good instructor? As they may be few and far between, this text can help bridge the gap by saving time and personal energy resources and avoiding costly errors incurred through ignorance.

In compiling this work, we have tried to anticipate and clarify gray areas which you, the reader, might incur in your efforts to relieve physical or emotional pain. However, as the title of this book indicates, healing the body is a mysterious thing and each case must be approached without ego projection. Instead, with the protection and guidance of Spirit and an honest and sincere effort, we hope this text will add to the building blocks of personal growth.

Karen Troiani
November 1996

ANCIENT MYSTERIES OF HEALING DISCOVERED

℃

Searching the Fringes of our Perceived Reality

We are now entering a time when humanity is beginning to accept the concept of a reality comprised of other dimensions beyond the common view of the physical universe. Slowly, we are identifying with the idea that each of us is a spirit and a soul housed in a physical body so that we can express ourselves in an earth plane existence.

According to their ancient Yoga philosophy, Hindus believe that the spirit and soul of a person lives forever through many reincarnations on the earth plane as well as other planes of reality on its journey to oneness with God. Through my years of research work with the human energy systems, I must agree with the Yoga principles. The primary spirit-soul body is identified with the auric energy system and the physical body is a manifestation or mirror image of the energy system.

The energy system, or aura fields, while carrying the composite signature of the body, is somewhat free to surround and penetrate the physical body. It is like a vapor surrounding the body and provides programmed energy to the physical part. See Figure 1.

After some years of dowsing experience, I found I could detect and accurately measure the aura fields surrounding the body. By scanning the fields with my dowsing rod, I could detect distortions and anomalies in the aura.

Beyond this point, I want to assure the readers that I am not attempting to alter their established beliefs with regard to religion, science or logic. The experiences described are my own and are supported in many cases with documentation.

The human entity is comprised of two primary intelligent spiritual and physical elements as it is related to the three-

4

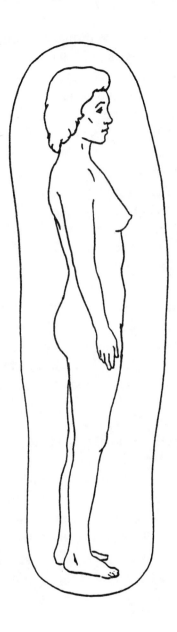

Figure 1:

dimensional earth plane. The primary system through which the three-dimensional physical element evolves is the multidimensional spiritual energy. This primary element is essentially invisible to us and commonly referred to as the aura. It is apparent that all forms of nature are a three-dimensional physical representation of their energy systems. Based on the acceptance of this concept of reality, we can now conclude that changes in the non-physical energy element will cause a change in the physical element and vice versa. These two primary elements effectively mirror each other.

Dowsing the Depths of Reality

Over the past several years, I have been actively researching psychic phenomena and the relationship of this phenomena to the dowsing ability. Evidence has shown that we are rediscovering a powerful facet of human ability, a dormant sense which, when activated, expands our conscious view of reality.

AN OVERVIEW OF THE DOWSING PHENOMENON

The art of dowsing /divining has been rediscovered but is not new. Reference to its use has been traced back to man's earliest recorded history. One of the earliest recorded uses of the divining rod is depicted on the walls of caves in North Africa and Spain. The drawings are estimated to be 3000-5000 years old. They depict a human figure holding a divining rod as though in search of water. In the study of mythology and ancient Zoroaster and Egyptian stone art, dowsing activities are often shown and sometimes reveal new techniques and uses for dowsing in spiritual ways. The wise men, shaman and magi of ancient tribes and cultures used dowsing to obtain insight and information to foretell and predict dangers and things to come.

So called "non-civilized" tribes in remote areas of the world are still practicing dowsing today as an accepted part of daily life.

Dowsing is the use of an inherent mental process. It is a latent mental sense that everybody has the ability to develop. An experienced dowser can excite the mental processes simply by focusing on the object of search and need to know. The portion of the mind which senses the dowsing signal is not the logic mind or the five senses but the subconscious which has a much deeper access to a broad spectrum of information. This function appears to originate outside our reference to three-dimensional concepts of space/time. As we function in a dowsing state, physical dimensions of distance and time become altered or nonexistent.

Operating in two parallel states of mind (conscious - subconscious) which the dowser uses, we can mentally project anywhere we wish to go in the physical plane and either backward or forward with respect to linear earth time.

To initiate the dowsing process, several simple instruments can be used. The dowsing instrument is an extension of your body and causes an amplification and visual indication of body reactions which might not otherwise be detected due to limited sensitivity to the human auto-motor system. The physical response relating to the dowsing phenomenon is thought to be produced by interaction between the conscious and subconscious portions of the human mind. The conscious mind establishes the "object of search" and the "need to know" requirements. The subconscious mind then searches out the requested information and communicates it through physical responses produced in the dowsing tools. The tool serves as a sensitive instrument responding to subtle energies and relating them to the dowser through the physical senses of sight and touch such as the particular movement indicated through a dowsing rod or the pendulum.

Tools of the Dowser

The dowsing instrument provides the bridge or link between the subconscious, where information initiates, and the conscious mind where it is brought to physical reality. This is the system within us that translates conscious and subconscious thoughts into physical motion. The auto-motor response of your nervous system and muscle tissue (and possibly other unknown sensitivity) provides the signal that produces the dowsing action. A pre-arranged coded program interpreted through the dowsing instrument motion must be established mentally to obtain reliable intelligent information from the instrument. By following the same sequence through the dowsing program, a mental program is established.

Under proper conditions, any of the dowsing instruments can provide a communication channel between the conscious and subconscious parts of your mind. It might seem strange, however, most people do not develop a contact with their subconscious mind except sporadically in dreams or under hypnosis. The subconscious mind plays a key part in successful dowsing; therefore, it is important to establish a good working relationship with that part of yourself. To do this requires patience and training, because your subconscious mind communicates in primitive ways using a language of symbols, signs and pictures rather than a language of words.

The Y-rod is the basic tool which has been associated with water dowsing. The Y-rod is named for its shape like the letter Y. The Y-rod is made by cutting a Y-shaped branch from a young tree. Some dowsers believe the wood of a particular tree is important and may prefer to use peach, hazel, willow or other wood. My experience has been that they all perform equally well, including a Y-rod made from plastic or spring wire. The preference is up to you.

The Y-rod is held in a flexed manner so as to produce a slight tension of the arm muscles. As an underground water source is approached, the end of the Y-rod will begin to dip until it reaches a vertical downward position directly over the center of the vein or pool. The response for some people is opposite and the rod end will turn upward rather than down. This action is related to a little understood polarity factor in the human body and the dowsing energy involved. Reversing the rod by turning it over will often change the rod action from upward to the desired downward motion. With experience, you will find that the action can be reversed by a mental command.

The L-rods are another commonly used dowsing tool. The L-rod is shaped like the letter L. Two rods are often used when performing a search. However, in some work an experienced dowser may choose to use only one L-rod. Using the two L-rods when performing a search has the added advantage of providing a polarity factor to your search information. This added information is quite helpful in accurately pinpointing a location or the object of your search.

The L-rods are arranged to swing freely in their handles and when conducting a search are held like two pistols and tilted slightly downward. The L-rods will most often develop a polarity difference when one rod is in each hand. When introduced to an energy field set up by underground streams, pipes, etc., they will react to the energy field and its polarity by swinging either away from each other or towards each other as the energy field is entered into.

The action will be determined by the polarities established between the rods and your body. Interchanging the rods between right and left hands will often reverse the rod action. If, experimentally, the two rods are held in the same hand they will develop a single polarity and both will react the same when brought into a search field pattern. These are not hard, fast rules.

We are all different in varying degrees. Therefore, your personal response to dowsing tools must be discovered by you. In mastering your dowsing abilities you will have the power to change some of the rules of response to better fit the need.

The L-rods, as well as other dowsing tools, show a sluggish or slow response for students in the learning stages or even for experienced dowsers during the initial few minutes of the search. The size and weight of the L-rods will also affect their speed of response. Because of this delay, it is important to move slowly when performing a search - to allow time for the rods to fully respond. Through practice and experience, you will be able to recognize this delay action and make necessary compensation for it. As your dowsing proficiency increases the delay time will become greatly reduced.

A single L-rod can be used to obtain yes and no answers as well as numbers representing depth of water, flow rate, etc. Using a single L-rod held in front and pointing away from you is the zero reference point. The response action of the L-rod to the left or right determines yes or no. You must test yourself by experimenting with which hand provides the best response as well as the direction indicating yes and no.

Simple L-rods can be made using coat hanger wire with a 90° bend at about one-third the total length to form the handle. When held loosely, these rods will turn when a dowsing signal is received. Coat hangers made of wire can also be used in their original form as dowsing rods. In this case, they are loosely held with the hook facing forward.

Some dowsers prefer to use a straight rod or wand to search out water veins. The wand can be made from a thin, straight branch from a young tree. You may, by testing, have a preference in the type of wood you choose. The wand could also be made from an end section of a glass or bamboo fishing rod or a telescoping car antenna or a piece of spring wire. The wand is usually made to the dowser's preference but generally should be three to four feet long and one-quarter to one-half inch in diameter at the handle end. Some dowsers prefer a flexible wand which is used with a whipping action.

The wand, like a single L-rod, will tend to assume direction associated with a dowsing energy field. As you move the rod into the field, you will develop the feeling that some force, other than your own, is moving the end of the rod in a direction of the water vein or pipe, etc. A modified wand is also used by some dowsers as a depth counting tool when depth to the water vein is requested. This tool is fitted with a small weight at the small end and is called a "bobber" because of its bobbing motion when in use. The wand is held over the water vein and the number of times the bobber bobs is an indicator of the depth to the vein, in the increment of measurement you have chosen, such as feet or meters.

The wand can be carried along one's side, centered end to end to give balance, and lightly supported on the finger tips. This position will be less tiring when the water search involves tracing small veins over long distances to locate the best spot for a water well.

The wand, in my opinion, requires a high degree of dowsing skill to use successfully. You may wish to use the wand as a dowsing tool after you have established your skill with the L-rods, the Y-rod, and the pendulum.

The pendulum is one of man's oldest recognized tools. It has been used throughout history to establish building lines perpendicular to the earth's surface and also to regulate

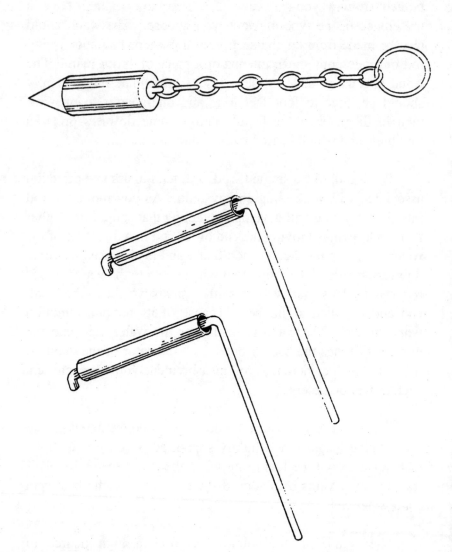

Figure 2:

mechanical motion in clocks. It, like the dowsing rods, develops motion under the influence of your auto-motor system activity, reacting with an energy force field generated by a water vein or other anomaly.

Through an understanding and translation of the pendulum's motion you can determine water location, depth, quality, flow-rate, as well as adding other new dimensions to your life. See Figure 2: L-rods and pendulum.

A simple pendulum can be made using a six inch length of string with a paper clip, washer, or button, acting as a weight attached to the end. Acting through your auto-motor system, the pendulum can provide "yes" or "no" answers to carefully phrased questions.

The pendulum's motion is influenced to a great degree by the earth's gravitational force. It will, without other influence, position itself perpendicular to the earth's surface. The dowser induces a subtle energy into the pendulum which causes it to move or gyrate about its gravitational center. These movements which are subconsciously induced into pendulum motion can be interpreted based on predetermined meanings such as "yes" or "no". The dowser is initiating the auto pendulum motion and watches for a sudden change in its motion as the indication or signal relating to his/her programmed search.

Typically, the clockwise-counterclockwise rotational movements of the pendulum are used to indicated polarity changes. It is important to train your subconscious to use the back and forth motion of the pendulum for "yes" and a crosswise motion to indicate "no". These pendulum movements might be reversed, but that does not present a problem as long as you know which is yes and no.

Begin by stating to yourself, "Please indicate a "yes"

action." If you find the pendulum does not move upon request, physically start the pendulum motion in back and forth or crosswise motions. Then repeat the yes and no questions. Take your time and maintain patience until you get reliable responses to the yes and no questions. Your sensitivity to the pendulum will increase as you work at it.

Where no answer to your question is available, the pendulum will either move back and forth at oblique angles or will rotate in an elliptical motion.

Becoming proficient with the pendulum or any of the dowsing tools requires much practice because you are communicating with your subconscious. It is best to practice a line of questioning to which someone can give you the correct answers. This will allow you to check your accuracy. You will be amazed how accurate the answers will be if you ask properly phrased questions which can only be answered with a yes or no. Do not allow your conscious mind to get into the act and destroy your efforts. Confusion indicated in the pendulum motion may relate to an element of time in the question; is it now? or in the future?

Once you have established your pendulum code, **do not change it**. To do so will lead to confusion of your subconscious—conscious mind relationship and may permanently damage your ability to use the pendulum.

The two most important conditions which must be established before any physical dowsing activity is begun are, **the need to know** and **the object of search**. To begin, you must establish a need to know which will physically and psychically motivate you to proceed. This motivation will come from wanting to help others or to demonstrate your new-found dowsing ability. The object of search in dowsing may be a vein of water, the parameters of a geopathic field, or the aura around the human body. You can learn to locate archeological features or objects, chart exact locations of burial sites in an ancient cemetery or find your way on a road map if you are lost. There are no limits to the application of dowsing in everyday life other than those of your imagination and belief in your own success.

Much of the dowsing phenomena and its related energy remains a mystery. Everyone has the inborn ability to dowse, but not everyone has an equal sensitivity to dowsing energy. This might be related to conscious attitudes, ability to communicate with the subconscious, body chemistry or other factors. Dowsing is a mental exercise which uses portions of the mind which are normally not utilized as activities of the five physical senses of sight, smell, taste, hearing and touch. In dowsing, these five senses, or at least some of them are used to relay to the conscious or logic mind the signal or response of the dowser's instrument. The logic mind, functioning on the physical earth plane, then evaluates the dowsing signal based on its stored data of learned information. This allows the dowser to evaluate the dowsing instrument response and develop a mental picture or concept of what exists beyond what can be detected by the five senses. It is very similar to our abilities using radar equipment to see and translate visible displays on a radar screen into meaningful information. Therefore, in the dowsing mode, our mind is functioning like a radar system only with much greater potential than radar with its defined limitations.

Based on a sampling of people who have attempted dowsing for the first time, I have found thirty percent show a reasonably high sensitivity at the first try, fifty percent show some response, and twenty percent show no response. Because you are communicating with your subconscious mind, the mental attitude of your conscious mind is critical to success. Those who believe that dowsing works without reservation have a high degree of success. Those who believe it is possible and

Sacred Yogis Symbols and Sounds

Mantras used to balance the body/mind
Aum - Center between the eyebrows
Ham - Throat center
Yam - Heart center
Ram - Navel center
Vam - Base of the spine
Lam - Base of the spine
(English translation of A is pronounced ah)

Figure 3:

Chakra Energy System

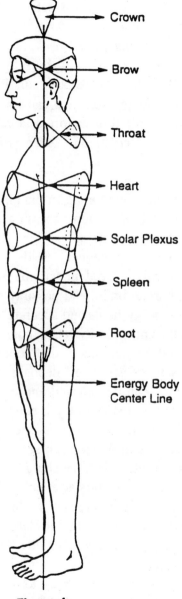

Crown

Brow

Throat

Heart

Solar Plexus

Spleen

Root

Energy Body
Center Line

Figure 4:

could work have moderate success followed by increased success as confidence builds. Those who do not believe it possible have great difficulty in opening their minds and will have little or no success in achieving a dowsing response. Those who cannot achieve a dowsing response are often "locked out" because of educational background based on the physical world or limitations imposed by religious dogma, doctrine or individual belief. There are conditions associated with a person's aura energy field that can limit their dowsing ability. People with a shifted or distorted aura field may find dowsing difficult. *See page 33, Aura Field Measurement and Evaluation.*

The dowser, functioning in the physical world of reality, is a translator of information accessing another level of mind. Dowsing energy appears to be a form of cosmic reactive energy similar to the earth's magnetic fields which permeates the earth and all physical material in varying strengths and vibrational rates. The human brain, and possibly other aspects of life, can detect these energy fields and accurately determine variations in their strength and polarity. Openings in the earth's sub-strata (either natural or man-made) that contain water or minerals, or in some instances gas or oil deposits, reflect particular energy patterns which can be detected and mapped by dowsing. This same application relates to the human body and the location of anomalies or distortions in the energy field surrounding the body. A competent dowser can scan the aura field with the L-rod or pendulum to locate the source of discomfort or disease in the physical body which is a reflection in physical matter of the energy patterns of the aura surrounding it. The energy systems or "chakras" can be evaluated to determine their vitality level. The term "chakra" comes from the Sanskrit word for wheel. These subtle energy vortices connect to endocrine glands and major nerve centers in the body as well as extending outward through the aura energy fields. See Figures 3 and 4.

18

Dr. Edith Jurka and the Mind Mirror

A number of years ago, Dr. Edith Jurka, a psychiatrist in New York City, attended the American Society of Dowsers Convention in Vermont with the intent to measure the dowser's brain wave patterns using a portable electronic instrument called a "mind mirror". See Figure 5. The upper display patterns of the instrument shown on the chart represents various states of brain activity through the frequency range in Hz. The lower display shows test results obtained in measuring brain activities of three different mental states: transcendental meditation (TM), zen meditation, and the dowser in an active state of dowsing. While the TM and zen meditation states are similar and are confined to the Alpha-Theta ranges, the dowser has a much larger alpha level while showing an expanding delta brain activity both in the beta (conscious) level as well as the delta sleep range.

The general conclusion from these tests was that the dowser is using a much broader spectrum of brain potential in his activities of information search than the average person uses in performing daily activities.

I attribute much of the information described in this publication to the mental processes attributed to dowsing such as the discovery of measurements of anomalies in the human aura energy fields and past life research work.

A Deep Search for Self

The story of dowsing, paranormal experiences, and psychic healing experiences which are about to unfold were experienced over a period of thirty years beginning in 1966. I have temporarily stopped time to write this book even though new experiences continue to occur. It is my responsibility to provide

19

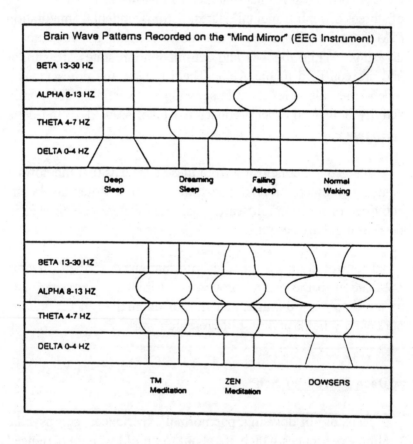

Figure 5:

20

the background and substantiating data as my contribution to humanity. It is an attempt to bring about a deeper understanding of human reality; a part of our reality we know little or nothing about. When prodded by friends to get started on this book, I was reluctant to write until I had experienced it all. I soon learned in my psychic research that I would never experience it all. Life is a perpetual learning and sorting process. It is a process of evaluating experiences and applying reason and logic to determine where they fit in this new perception of reality.

When I was introduced to the phenomenon of dowsing, I was amazed to find that the dowsing instruments moved independently as if by a magical force. As a small child of five or six, I accompanied my father as he would search for a source of potable water for friends and neighbors who had problems with their well or had purchased property that needed a well. At that young age, I was curious but not curious enough to try it for myself.

The next time I was exposed to the dowsing phenomenon was in 1966. This was the beginning of an avocation which over a period of thirty years has evolved into a full time research program with many exciting discoveries and experiences.

My background was quite average for the times. I graduated from high school at the height of World War II, was drafted and spent three years in the US Army as a medical technician in the 197th general hospital in France. After returning from the service, I was hired by the General Electric Company in their locomotive division in my home town of Erie, Pennsylvania.

One day a co-worker brought a pair of L shaped dowsing rods to work. It was a great curiosity in the office during the lunch hour. We decided to try them out in the parking lot. We decided to search for the water pipe connecting two fire hydrants. When it was my turn to try the rods, I wasn't quite sure what to expect. I moved slowly through the area between the two hydrants, and much to my surprise, the ends of the rods began to move away from each other and at one location were pointing in opposite directions. This was the center of the water pipe. It was a very strange experience because the rods moved as if by magic without the sensation that I was causing it to happen. I was merely an observer.

I spent a great deal of time trying to bring this experience into the scope of accepted science. I made and experimented with many types of dowsing instruments trying to find the secret of their response. In one experiment, I attached two L-rods to the handlebars of a bicycle and pushed the bicycle through my yard in an area where there were known water veins under ground. This test showed no response from the L-rods and revealed the fact that I had to be holding the rods in order to get a reaction from them. I was part of the phenomenon.

Stimulated by even greater curiosity to know more about this phenomenon, I spent a great deal of time dowsing around the house for pipes and water veins. My neighbor, who had purchased the vacant lot nearby, called to ask if I would dowse his land for a location to drill a successful water well.

I tried to assure him that I was not a professional dowser, but a novice with no credentials or prior experience. It seemed like a great opportunity, but I realized that it carried some responsibility if I should fail. With more prodding and persuasion I agreed to search the property for a reliable source of potable water.

I developed a plan of search that incorporated my best logical thinking coupled with the information I obtained by reading the movements of the dowsing rods. Attempting to leave no stone unturned and assure success of my first dowsing project, I drove many stakes in the ground over indications of water veins as I slowly walked the lines of a grid pattern I had laid out on the property. When complete, the overall arrangement of the stakes presented an outline on the surface representative of the arrangement of a number of water veins flowing at a depth of twenty-five feet below the surface. Using a combination of logic and dowsing information, a spot was marked where the well should be placed to obtain the highest flow rate of potable water.

The well was dug and as predicted, at twenty-five feet, the vein was reached and water rushed into the well. The well has continuously provided an abundant supply of clear water. I now had proof that the dowsing phenomena was a reality and that I had the ability to use this newly discovered sense; a sense which allows us to see the unseen and explore realms of new and expanded dimensions.

Each water dowsing job was unique to the particular character of the land. Dowsing information provided the key data which produced successful water wells and continued to build a high degree of confidence that dowsing was a practical and reliable technique of searching out the unknown.

My conscious mind was not as quick to accept these dowsing experiences as fact. With a background in electrical engineering and having spent my entire life to this point working within the limits of the five sense world, my logic mind had many questions about the reality of the dowsing phenomena. I conducted many tests using experimental dowsing instruments in a variety of situations.

In the early stages of my research into dowsing, I thought I was pretty much alone in my interest. I didn't know any active dowsers. Some people would remember their grandfather or uncle who could dowse for water, but beyond the search for water, there didn't seem to be any other kind.

In the local newspaper, I saw an advertisement for a workshop on dowsing at the local college. This was my first opportunity to meet another dowser. The workshop leader was a dowser named Raymond Wiley. During the course of the workshop as he described theories, principles and techniques that dowsers use, he mentioned that he was a member of the American Society of Dowsers. Elated, I quickly filled out the application and joined the society so that I might meet and exchange experiences with other dowsers.

The American Society of Dowsers has grown to a membership of over four thousand. Society Conventions and Conferences are extremely valuable as they disseminate information on the diverse aspects of dowsing through lectures, workshops and schools on the subject. You can write for more information to: The American Society of Dowsers, P. O. Box 24, Danville, Vermont 05828-0024.

Another organization of significant interest is the Ozark Research Institute, P. O. Box 387, Fayetteville, Arkansas 72702-0387. ORI is a non-profit organization whose focus is to conduct research into the power of thought/power of mind and investigate all manner of mind phenomenon as well as healing techniques.

Progression into this new reality seemed to move in steps; first, a period of concentrated work in the area of water dowsing, learning the intricate details of the process which provided the greatest accuracy and selecting the instrument which was most reliable in producing accurate information. Then, translating principles of water dowsing to other areas of interest such as measuring aura energy fields. I continued dowsing water wells with an acceptable accuracy of 98% and learned many critical idiosyncrasies of dowsing, each of which could make the difference between success and failure.

For instance, at a point in my research, I discovered there is an inherent error in locating the exact center of a water vein when approaching the vein from one side versus the other. For me, the error can vary between four and ten inches. Correction for this error can easily be made by approaching the vein from each side, marking the center from each side, then taking one half the difference as the true center. This could be quite critical if the water vein was in a narrow, hard rock fracture and you planned to intersect it with an eight inch diameter hole at a significant depth.

Water dowsing, like other forms of searching, requires patience and continued testing of the information until you have generated a logical picture to satisfy your search. Your first attempts at water dowsing will likely leave you with a feeling of conscious doubt and insecurity. This is normal, as in any new adventure, when you have not had previous experience. Remember, you are working with an energy medium. Do not become discouraged because of mistakes, admit them to yourself and add them to your experience records.

It will take time to develop your dowsing skills. Be conservative in your work. Rely on the indications of your dowsing instrument. Do not get over-anxious and do not allow wishful thinking or someone else's ideas to confuse your logic. Remember, you are in control and working with an energy medium that most people cannot even comprehend.

Dowsing activities being of a psychic nature can be strenuous and tiring. As you become mentally tired you will find a significant drop in your dowsing abilities. When this point is reached you should discontinue the activity until you are rested. Failure to do so can lead to unnecessary mistakes. Consider your dowsing abilities as a gift of God or a higher divine power. Treat it with reverence and use it only with a good purpose in mind. Ask for divine guidance if you feel it is necessary.

Recognition and control of your conscious ego is very important in dowsing. The ego can interfere with or destroy your dowsing ability. To maintain your concentration and overcome any self-consciousness you may have, it is best that you work through your experiments alone taking your time. The ego tends to distort the dowsing program particularly when you are emotionally involved with the outcome. In an emotionally charged situation, it is best to call in another qualified dowser.

As my dowsing research work continued, I began to realize the importance of developing an accurate visualization of the unseen; a mental picture based on signals emanating from the dowsing instrument.

Noxious (Geopathic) Fields

The earth is permeated by cosmic energy and powerful electromagnetic forces which are continually changing and rebalancing themselves. Very little research has been done to identify the nature of these fields and their effect on the human body.

Noxious fields are thought to emanate from underground streams and geological stresses and rock faults deep in the earth's crust. Because of their strange nature, it is presently impossible to detect these energy fields with common scientific measuring equipment. Scientific research indicates that noxious fields might be detectable through their distorting effects on the

26

earth's magnetic field, which can be readily measured using a magnetometer. The noxious field can be detected by dowsing. The noxious fields affect the dowsing device similarly to the rod action noted when dowsing for flowing water. It is important to differentiate between noxious fields and water veins when searching for water.

Noxious fields have the interesting characteristic that they typically run in fairly straight lines with an occasional oblique angled turn here and there. They are of random lengths, from a few inches up to miles in length. This is the characteristic used by the dowser to identify the noxious field from water veins, which have a meandering characteristic similar to a river or stream on the earth's surface.

Noxious fields are sometimes found crossing each other or a noxious water vein. This condition is a most dangerous situation with respect to body damage because of the added effects of the two or more fields interacting with each other. In less common cases, noxious energy fields are found in the form of a cyclonic vortex spinning either clock-wise or counter-clockwise, much like a tornado. These fields are dangerous to live in because they alter the physical as well as the auric energy field of living things. One example of the damaging nature of the noxious field is the spiral twist in the trunks of trees trying to grow within the geopathic field.

The human body responds to noxious field energy in a variety of ways. In children, the symptoms are often indicated by sleeplessness, hypertension, bed wetting and nightmares. It appears that the noxious field energies are reacting with the child's nervous system and the brain to produce over-activity of various glands and organs, as well as preventing the brain from shifting to the delta sleep range.

Severe cases of noxious field effects can result in a reduction of the aura fields around the body to 4-5 inches or less, producing symptoms such as depression, hypertension, anxiety, nervous tension, or in later stages, a gaunt look with a suppressed or introverted personality. Loss of feeling and motor control, beginning in the extremities have been evident after long term exposure to noxious field energy.

Not all energy fields are noxious or damaging to the body. There are energy fields which appear to be of opposite polarity to the noxious fields and stimulate human auric energy that surrounds the body. These areas were treated as sacred by primitive people and ancient cultures including the Native Americans who built stone circles over them.

There is a simple test to see how the field affects a person's aura. To determine whether the field is noxious (negative) or positive, measure a person's aura with the dowsing instrument as he/she stands outside the field. Then measure it again as he/she stands in the energy field. It is important that the person taking the aura measurement is not in the noxious field at any time while measuring to prevent erroneous readings. If the aura reduces in size when the person is standing within the field, this indicates a noxious effect. The person may also show indications of discomfort or dizziness after a short time in the field.

Two effective ways of dispersing noxious fields passing through a house are: (1) by driving iron rods into the ground where the field is; or (2) surrounding the house, the room, or the bed with a copper wire loop allowing a six inch gap in the loop.

The rod approach is the quickest way to resolve the noxious field problem. However, its long lasting effect might be limited by field shifting within the earth which can be caused by moon cycles, etc. Placement of the rods is quite critical and, therefore, any field shift can make them ineffective.

The copper wire loop is easy to apply and you need not be a professional dowser or have any technical background.

Use single insulated or bare #12 or #14 copper house wire to surround the area to be protected from the noxious fields. The wire can be fastened in place using small staples. In arranging the copper loop, it is important that a 6-inch opening is left between the two ends. It is also important that the ends be stapled or taped to a stick or board to maintain their alignment facing each other.

The copper wire loop can be attached to the lower edge of the box spring, if clearing fields from only the bed. If the room is to be cleared of noxious fields, then a larger wire loop should be attached around the baseboard or to the floor, again, leaving the 6-inch gap at the open ends of the loop.

For further reading on the subject, refer to my book entitled, *Noxious (Geopathic) Fields Are Damaging To Your Health*, 1993, ISBN: 0-9652547-0-4.

Welcome to Your Aura

There is a spiritual and non-physical intelligent energy principle associated with the human body called the aura. The aura permeates and projects beyond the physical body. Perhaps more accurately, the physical body is a projection of the aura. It is the energy that provides vitality or fuel to power the physical aspects of the body, brain and nervous system. This energy has been recognized from ancient times as the primary energy source supporting the physical manifestation in the three-dimensional earth plane.

We exist as both energy and intelligence. The Yoga philosophy teaches that, "The physical body is built up of cells, each cell containing within it a miniature 'life', which controls its action. These 'lives' are really bits of intelligent mind of a certain degree of growth, which enable the cells to perform their work properly." Cellular organizations also form a group mind of intelligence leading to the complex functions of all aspects of the human body. There is every reason to believe that we can communicate with our cells. Cellular communication can be accomplished through manipulation and stimulation of the aura energy fields.

The aura is a composite envelope of energy fields surrounding and permeating the physical body. The auric energy which projects to the body carries the programs and energies which manifests the characteristics evident in the physical form.

Those who have the ability to see auras can identify three fields in various colors. It is likely that the projection of auras range beyond the three most often identified, which we can't perceive because of our limited ability to sense their presence.

The auras combined have an overall function to energize each of our millions of cells with a coded program which enables them to perform their specific functions to support our physical form as a whole.

The three aura fields surrounding the body have a relationship to each other as well as to the physical body. They reflect anomalies in the physical body as well as in each other. When scanning the outermost of the three fields, if a hole or energy void is located, it will project through all three fields to a specific or general area of the body. See Figure 6. A physical injury such as a broken bone might have happened years earlier but the memory and the effect of it will remain imprinted in the energy aura resulting in a chronic condition of pain, numbness, loss of control or other symptoms such as sensitivity to barometric pressure change associated with changing weather.

Configuration of the Human Aura Energy Fields

The three auric energy fields permeate the physical body and appear to have a common central axis within the body. They project externally from the body and are physically measurable outside the body using a dowsing procedure. The field closest to the body which I will arbitrarily call the **etheric field** is the most dense of the three beyond our physical body. The etheric body has the radiated essence of heat and smell and closely follows the contours of the physical body. When brought into the visible spectrum, it appears as webs between the fingers filling the spaces between the fingers near their juncture with the main body of the hand. The etheric field may also be seen as a narrow black line just off the surface of the shoulders, often with small sparks moving along the field surface.

The middle auric field, arbitrarily called the **astral body**, is considerably less dense with respect to the etheric field. It is centered between the etheric and outer mental auric fields. This energy field is where much of a person's traumatic emotional energy programs are stored; possibly the home of the human spirit. This field, when its outer surface is scanned using a dowsing instrument, surrounds the physical body and follows major contours of the body but not the finer details found in the etheric field.

The outer aura, arbitrarily identified as the **mental body,** is progressively less dense with regard to the physical body and has almost no references to features of the physical body. It appears like a plastic dry cleaner bag suspended over and

31

Male - Aura fields showing depressions

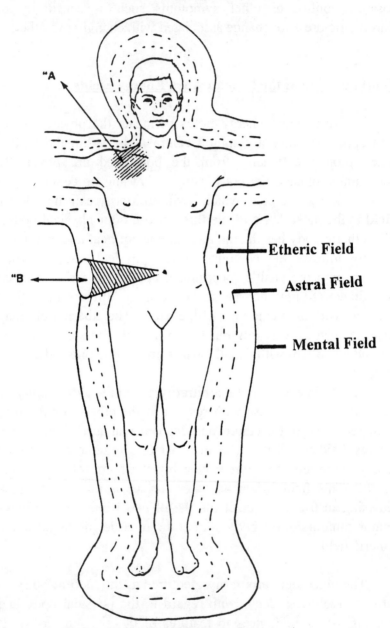

Ref. "A": Physical injury in shoulder area
Ref. "B": Hole in aura field indicating physical problem

Figure 6:

surrounding the physical body. The mental aura is furthest from the physical body and is much thinner than the inner two aura fields. This may be considered the home of the soul.

When viewed from the three-dimensional physical plane, the aura energy fields represent a transitional system between the physical state and the various states we refer to as spiritual.

Having had the opportunity to closely observe the process of a death transition, I found that the etheric energy field (closest to the physical body) withdrew from the physical body at least twelve hours before the observed physical death. The astral and mental energy fields withdrew in close progressive sequence at the point of death of the physical. At this point, the body became rigid and lifeless.

Aura Field Measurement and Evaluation

The aura fields surround the body form as an envelope. Or they can be visualized as layers of an onion with the physical body in the center. The health and quality of the aura fields are of primary importance to the health of the physical body. Many functional problems within the physical body including its mental aspects are associated with anomalies in the aura fields.

Shifted and distorted aura fields as well as holes in the field can have the following observed effects.

1. Infertility, inability to conceive or successfully carry a pregnancy to term. The problem can also relate to a suppressed past life experience. This may involve the energy fields of both male and female.

2. Dyslexic characteristics in varying degrees.

33

3. Physical distortion of the body and chronic pain resulting in twitching or muscle spasms.

4. Vertigo or dizziness can be caused by shifted or distorted aura fields.

5. Migraine headaches are often caused by shifted or distorted aura fields.

6. Hypertension, TMJ and attention span disorders are often caused by shifted aura fields resulting in imbalances of the brain functions.

7. Instability of male/female relationships can occur due to altered personalities from field shifts.

The three fields closest to and permeating the physical body, while separated from each other, are connected through their energy relationships and respond together through the energy system. Anomalies found in one field will also be present in the other two. See Fig. 7.

The outer (mental/emotional body) is best to work with because it has a relatively smooth surface and does not conform to the contours of the physical body. In scanning the surface of the outer field it is important to first determine how well the field is centered by measuring distance between the physical body and the edge of the outer field using an L-rod and a stiff measuring tape to record the reading. Take and record measurements about waist high on front, back, left side and right side. Then have the person lie horizontally and measure the aura at the head and feet. See Fig. 8.

Aura field shifts are common and affect the overall functional balance of the physical/mental body. They can produce many unusual and chronic problems in the physical

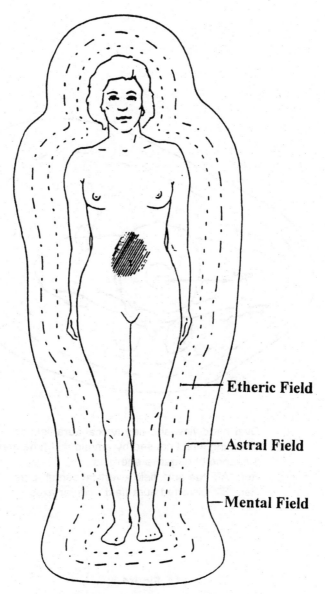

Etheric Field

Astral Field

Mental Field

Ref. "A": Female - Solar plexus chakra shut
down causing hole in the aura. Possible cause -
trama or presence of negative energy.

Figure 7:

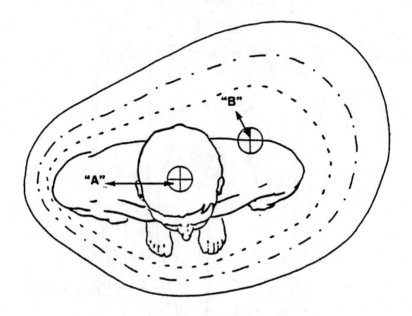

Over head view showing typical aura field shift and
blooming effect caused by emotional trama and
presence of negative energies.
Ref. "A": true aura field - vertical center axes.
Ref. "B": Distorted aura field - center axes.

Figure 8:

body. One interesting affect of aura field shifting is what I call the "Blooming Effect." The aura shift will produce a blooming or expanding characteristic on the large side of the field. The aura field measurements will add up to a much larger number than would be found in measuring a balanced aura field.

Through accumulation of data, I have found that statistically, side shifts are more prevalent and severe than front to back shifts. Left shifts are more common than right shifts by about 75%. Back shifts are more common than front shifts by about 90%. Single shifts where the aura field is shifted in only one plane are rare but do occur.

The overall effect of various combinations of shifts is extremely complex. However, a number of common problems can result from field shifts. The severity of the physical problem is associated directly with the combination and severity of the shifts. Physical distortion of the body and associated problems become more intense with greater degrees of field shift.

PROCEDURE:

Using a single small (six inch) dowsing L rod held about waist high, move slowly toward the client's body. See Fig. 9. State silently, "Please show me the surface of the mental (outer) aura projecting from this body." After a time you will have established a program in your mind and the program will automatically be present without the requesting statement.

The L-rod end should be held just slightly tilted down and pointing at the body. You should begin the search at a distance of three or four feet from the body. Moving slowly, search for the place where the L-rod abruptly moves to the left or right reaching a position parallel to the body at a distance from it. This action will locate the surface of the outer aura, the mental/emotional body. After the six measurements have been taken (front, back, left & right sides, head & foot) and recorded, begin scanning the outer field looking for holes and depressions in the field. When a hole in the field is approached, the L-rod will suddenly drop into the void pointing at the body and will quickly return to the position parallel to the body when the hole is passed. A depression will be indicated where the L-rod moves to a position between parallel to the body (100% aura) and straight in, 0% aura. With a little experience you can estimate the percentage of missing aura by dividing the 90° quadrant of rod movement into four quarters, i.e, half way in would be 50% etc. See Figure 10. This information is of interest to the researcher but is not really important to know for healing purposes.

It is important to become familiar with holding the L-rod just slightly tilted downward during the scanning sweeps over the aura otherwise, due to weight shift as you move, the L-rod movement will become erratic. It will take practice and time to master the L-rod use.

Scan the aura on the body front and back three times sweeping slowly over the surface of the aura from the neck down at the center and at each side of center. Then, do the same on the back. Then sweep each side from top to bottom. The head should be scanned separately, front, back, left and right. It is important to move slowly to allow the L-rod time to respond to anomalies. As you become more proficient with continued practice, the L-rod response will become faster and your accuracy will continually improve. Where a depression is found while scanning the side of the body, it will be necessary to have the person raise their arm to determine if the anomaly is in the arm or in the torso.

A hole or depression in the aura fields is an indication of a problem in the physical body. It might be the imprint left by an

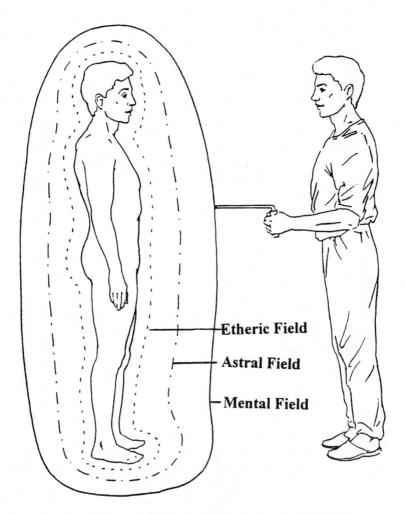

Etheric Field

Astral Field

Mental Field

Scanning the surface of the aura fields using the dowsing "L" rod.

Figure 9:

39

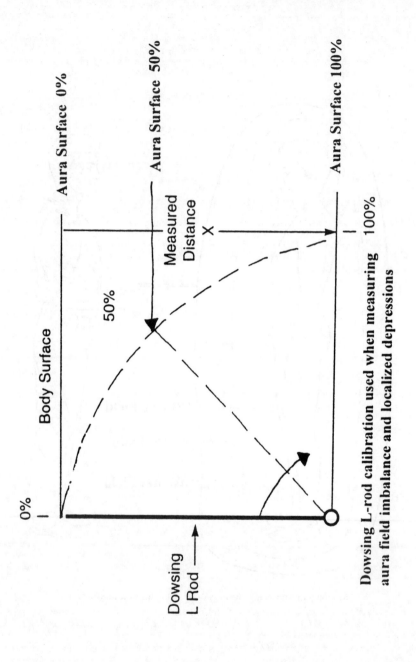

Figure 10:

40

injury or broken bone which occurred many years earlier or it might be a physical problem which is in process but hasn't yet progressed to the stage of discovery in the physical body.

The Yogis believe that all physical problems and diseases, except accidents, have their beginnings in the aura energy fields.

The presence of spirit possession by negative energies can also result in holes in the aura fields if they are present and localized in a particular area. It appears that the negative energies have a polarity that is opposite to ours thus canceling out or neutralizing our aura field energy in the area where they are present. Often negative energies are dispersed throughout the aura field rather than concentrated. Their presence is also responsible for off center shifts in the aura fields. The human spirit associated with an abortion or miscarriage, if present, will be indicated by a hole in the aura in the spleen or solar plexus area (second or third chakra). If present, it must be treated differently than any other causes of holes in the aura. With approval, the client can be guided through a procedure of release.

Aura Field Response to Charging and Manipulation

The aura energy fields surrounding and permeating the human body behave like an electrostatic energy system in resonance. Altering a person's energy system by manipulation, or adding energy within the auric envelope surrounding the physical body can cause temporary loss of equilibrium and nausea. Adding energy to the system stimulates cellular activity which is often expressed as improved sight, hearing, or clearer thinking. Stimulation of the cellular functions through manipulation of the energy fields results in rapid healing processes to the point of occurring almost instantly in various experiences. Adding energy to the auric system also effects a

41

removal of pain caused by damaged or distressed nerves or tissue. This method of removing pain and stimulating healing processes has a significant effect on minimizing injury trauma.

To transfer auric energy from one person to another requires that you first, locate and engage a source of energy to draw from and second, focus your mental intent to direct the energy to the person in need of it. Either left or right hand can be used to draw energy. Physical movements of the hands or fingers can be used to initiate the healing or energy transfer. For transferring energy to large areas or the overall body the open hand can be used with quick packing-type motions like packing snow when building a snowman or making snowballs. It is not necessary to touch the physical body when working in the aura energy fields.

Directing the healing energy to fill holes in specific areas of the aura can be accomplished using the fingers and especially the index finger. The energy flow can often be seen and in extreme cases where a large potential difference exists between the healer and the client an electrical spark discharge will be observed and sometimes felt. This phenomenon is felt as a tingling of the finger tips when holding the small L-rod and scanning the aura field of another person or as a mild electrical shock.

It is important to super charge the aura field to ensure sufficient energy to complete the physical healing. An inadequate charge of healing energy will result in an incomplete physical healing. Excess energy beyond that needed to complete the physical healing process will be indicated by an extremely large aura surrounding the person after the field stabilizes. The excess energy will slowly dissipate over several days to reach a normal balance.

Etheric Life Energy Sources

Within the three-dimensional physical plane, our bodies are renderings of an organized energy system which is associated with what we have identified as the aura fields surrounding and permeating the physical body. Included in the aura field system is a chakra system where the energy is transformed from etheric energies to the physical. See Figure 4 on page 17. The chakra system appears as fixed harmonic energy nodes related to the base line frequency of our physical body.

Many sources of the special life force energy is available and called by many different names throughout recorded history. Today, it is commonly called 'auric energy' as a generic term. It was also referred to as 'odic force' by Karl Von Reichenbach, an eighteenth century famous German chemist. The Yogi's of India call it 'prana'. Wilhelm Reich, a famous American researcher called it 'orgon' energy. The Huna healers of the Polynesian Islands in the Pacific called it 'mana'. Its presence and nature was obviously well known by ancient man. The shaman and healers around the world were well versed in its nature, use and how to draw on its source for healing purposes.

There are many sources of auric energy available from the sun, foods and the cosmos that surround and penetrate our bodies as the auric field envelope. It is important that you do not knowingly give your personal auric energy away to someone who is depleted and in need of energy. Unless you are a practicing healer with the knowledge of how to retain a large reserve of auric energy you can quickly become depleted. Certain people have the ability to draw auric energy from you without your awareness or understanding of what is happening. You recognize a loss of energy in the presence of this energy type. You can also be unaware in the conscious mind that you are giving your auric energy away by showing sympathy or deep emotional concern toward someone experiencing health problems or death. It is important to do what you can too help someone but recognize a limit to giving your auric energy. Each of us must experience our lives from birth through death as the spiritual plan unfolds. Therefore, there are limits to what you can do for someone else. Your presence or thoughts may be all that is required of you.

It is important to recognize that there are a number of sources of auric energy oriented in the cosmos where energy can be drawn from. I call them 'hot spots' as they will produce the sensation of heat or tingling in the palm of the hand when the outstretched hand is searching for them. There is a powerful system in the cosmos oriented to the geometry of the Star of David, the hexagram. It is a primary system which provides an abundant supply of auric field energy that flows to us naturally from the source and can be directed or channeled by mental intent. The overall system can be viewed as a series of tuning forks or energy transmitters resonating at specific frequencies that our bodies resonate with. This is much like tuning your radio to a far off radio station. The flow of auric field energy is not impeded by three-dimensional solid objects including the earth. It can be concluded that it originates from a source outside our three-dimensional concept of reality. While there are random focused sources of this energy in the cosmos, the system is the primary life support for all life forms on earth.

Locating Your Etheric Energy Source

When I began my healing work I had a natural inclination to receive healing energy from a source before I could pass it on to a client. In searching around with my hand open like an antenna I found there were 'hot spots' where I could feel strong tingling sensations in my hands and body. I access this source as the limitless supply of auric energy to supercharge a client's energy field and improve their health.

Later on in my research work through a healer friend, I discovered the presence of what appears to be a primary energy system in space, or possibly in another dimension, which provides tremendous quantities of auric field energy and raised my healing abilities by more than 100 times. I became aware that in certain cases where a client had a severely depleted aura it was necessary to limit the energy flow to control the healing process within physical limits. The presence of this system provides an unlimited source of healing energy anywhere on earth. It is the energy that vitalizes the human body and other living forms.

This super energy system is a resonating energy form in the shape of a six pointed hexagram. It has been symbolized since ancient times in the form of two identical equilateral triangles arranged with a common center. ✿ The symbol is identified throughout history as Solomon's Seal, The Shield of David (Magin David) and in the Yoga philosophy, the heart chakra symbol identified with a twelve petaled lotus flower and the Sanskrit sound YAM.

The six sided energy resonance identified with a hexagram transposes to many forms within nature. Snow flakes which form from water in the atmosphere also display the hexagonal geometry. Honey bees in their evolution also found the hexagram to be the most efficient geometric design in storing their honey. They are obviously programmed throughout the world to construct the six sided hexagon. The geometric form is repeated many times over through the micro/macro span of nature. It can therefore be viewed as a natural force to which certain physical material will respond and conform. Through research and experience I view the energy which generates the hexagonal form as very basic to forms of life activity on our planet and possibly others in the physical universe. The macro system in present times has been called the etheric or planetoid fields. These energy fields can be visualized as six individual tuning forks; each vibrating in harmonic resonance with the hexagonal geometry of the whole, thus providing the seventh point of resonance in the center of the geometric figure.

The hexagon is a natural geometric figure produced by dividing the circumference of a circle by its radius. The points on the circumference are connected by straight lines, making a figure with six equal sides. The hexagon's direct relationship to the circle is allied with another property in which the alternate vortices of the figure are joined by straight lines to produce a hexagram. This figure composed of interpenetrating equilateral triangles symbolizes fusion of opposite principles: male and female, hot and cold, water and fire, earth and air, etc., and is consequently symbolic of the archetypal whole, the divine power of creation. It was used in alchemy and is a sacred symbol of the Jewish people to this day.

The quartz crystal, a three-dimensional hexagram which grows under the influence of the earth's natural electromagnetic resonating energy system, displays a number of very interesting characteristics commonly referred to as the "pizo-electric effect." If subjected to physical distortion it will produce an electrical impulse. If subjected to a pulsing electromagnetic field it will slightly expand physically and in thin sections will vibrate at a fixed resonant frequency. This principal is applied to radio and electronic devices including your battery powered watch.

The etheric fields are approximately 20° clockwise on the compass with respect to the cardinal points as shown in Figure 11. They move slightly in a cyclic pattern which I attribute to earth rotation.

The Geometry Of Life

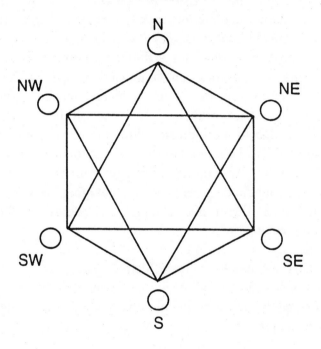

Figure 11:

These fields can best be located by dowsing. Using the L-rod, ask to be shown your etheric field energy source and slowly turn your body on its vertical center while holding a single L-rod in front of you. When you contact the particular direction of your etheric field the L-rod will lock onto it and will not follow your rotation. When this point has been found, move back slightly until you are directly facing the direction of your energy source and the L-rod is facing directly away from your body. Noting the direction, slowly raise your hand, palm open, fingers spread like an antenna. Experimentally determine which hand works best. Feel for a tingling sensation, heat, cold, or other strange sensations in your hand or body which will be obvious when you are on the field and receiving the etheric energy. There is a primary field which will be the strongest on a vertical line in the indicated direction of your etheric field. There will also be secondary harmonics found at points on the vertical line. Any of these energy sources are suitable for charging your field. To enhance the charging, take several deep breaths, then direct and channel the energy to the person needing healing.

This system is very effective and may produce heat sensations in the person receiving the charge. The charging can be slowed by temporarily moving your hand off the etheric energy source.

It is not a good idea to charge yourself using the etheric field source and not direct its flow to someone else. As your energy builds to a higher and higher level, you may feel spacey and light headed. Should this happen, crossing your arms or legs will short circuit and discharge the excess energy down to your normal aura energy level.

The pendulum can also be used to search out your etheric energy field. Look for a reverse of pendulum rotation when you pass through it. The pendulum will give two indications 180°

apart. It will be necessary to determine whether it is in front or behind you by asking, "Is my etheric energy source located in this direction? That direction?"

The geometry of the double triangle, if properly made of physical material, will automatically resonate with the energy spectrum of the hexagonal geometry. Experimentally, I have found that the double triangle, if properly made and programmed, will perform as a miniature resonator (tuning fork) and, if in physical contact with the body, will stimulate the body aura field through resonance with the micro/macro system, thus significantly stimulating all aspects of physical health. I have coined the name ©ETHERIC TRANSPONDER (ET) to identify the instrument and its principles of operation.

I must caution that most of the Star of David symbols found in jewelry stores are strictly symbolic and do not perform as an ©ETHERIC TRANSPONDER although they look similar.

Aura Field Wave Propagation When Transferring Energy

It is not necessary to understand the energy transfer process to be a successful healer. However, if you have an interest in the nature of the process for research purposes I will include this information based on my research.

Directing energy into the human auric energy field tends to excite the overall system by energizing the millions of individual cells. The cells in turn respond by generating an energy wave response at a level nearly equal in strength to the initiating energy wave. The cellular response can vary from one person to another depending on the energetic level of a person's cells.

49

The energy system passes through two phases of wave propagation before stabilizing. After directing a charge of auric energy into the auric field of a person, the field when measured with the dowsing L-rod will begin to oscillate in a wave pattern between two points which I have identified as point "A" closest to the physical body and point "B" furthest from the body. See Fig. 12.

During the charging process, the aura fields expand and contract radiating in all directions from the physical body. The number of oscillations of the energy wave is determined by the strength of the charge and the response from the person's cells. Typically the response is between six and twelve wave cycles. The wave propagation will then revert to a secondary process beginning somewhere between points A and B.

I have termed the secondary phase as "Cellular Energy Absorption Phase". In this phase, the energy field will drop characteristic to that of a geometric progression. The sequence of rapid drops in the field energy will progress as one half of the previous drop until the field reaches a stable point which is most often at a dimension larger than the original aura surrounding the body. This depends to a great degree on how depleted the original field was at the beginning of the charging procedure. It might be necessary to repeat the charging procedure several times to initiate a high level of reserve cellular energy. Each time the energy field will progressively repeat the two stages. Most often, as the field energy builds to a higher level, the frequency of oscillations between points A and B will become more rapid and the stabilizing point will be double that of the previous charging. Often the stimulated cells will initiate an in-phase energy response wave and the energy balance point will be the product of the initiating energy plus the cellular generated energy.

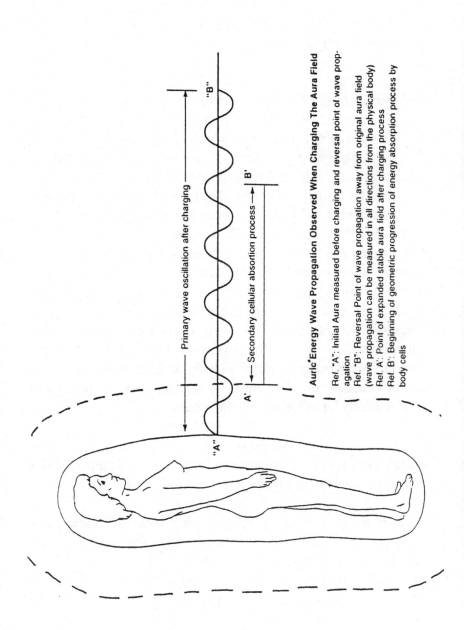

Auric Energy Wave Propagation Observed When Charging The Aura Field

Ref. "A": Initial Aura measured before charging and reversal point of wave propagation

Ref. "B": Reversal Point of wave propagation away from original aura field (wave propagation can be measured in all directions from the physical body)

Ref. A': Point of expanded stable aura field after charging process

Ref. B': Beginning of geometric progression of energy absorption process by body cells

Primary wave oscillation after charging

Secondary cellular absorption process

Figure 12:

51

During the charging programs the person might describe the sensation of heat or cold, nausea or dizziness which quickly passes as the energy stabilizes.

Healing Through Manipulation of the Auric Field

There are three aura fields which can be reliably measured. The combination of the three energy fields organizes cellular structures into the overall physical living structure. These fields can become damaged and distorted through physical accidents, mental or emotional distress or outside influences. The energy fields characteristically are locked together. Thus, distortion or holes found in one field will also project through the other two and into the physical body. The affects will result in distress or distortion in the physical body in the affected area. Many conditions which are mysterious and cannot be medically diagnosed are caused by aura field distortions. These effects can vary widely through the physical and mental aspects of the person. In essence, the physical body and the energy auras are mirror images of the other. An anomaly in one will automatically be reflected into the other.

Based on extensive personal research, I view the human energy system and its effects as an important missing part of our concept of human health and how our total system functions.

An interesting case, for example, was a middle aged woman I had the opportunity to work with. She had a tic in the left side of her face close to her eye. She said she had it for ten years and it was greatly limiting her life. The medical advice she received was to sever the affected nerve to eliminate the twitching. However there was the great possibility that the facial muscles would be affected and cause sagging or distortion of the face.

I was very interested in the condition of her aura field. She agreed to allow me to measure her aura with my dowsing rod. Upon scanning her field, I found it severely shifted both side to side and front to back. I didn't check for a vertical field shift but I suspect the aura was shifted vertically also. The side shift was to the right with the smaller field on the affected side. The front to back shift was to the back which is most common. I then checked her for what I call "negative energies" and the number was eighteen, a sizable number on my scale. I discussed the process of clearing and she agreed with the procedure to perform the clearing. As I progressively removed the negatives, the twitching became less and less and when we had cleared all but the last one the twitching had subsided to only extremely small ripples in the tissue in the affected area. The final clearing removed all traces of the original ten-year-old twitching problem. The complete process took less than thirty minutes. It was several hours before she realized that this long standing problem was no longer present. This commonly occurs because the conscious mind is not participating in the process and therefore must discover the change through the five senses.

I was fascinated witnessing the change in the woman's face with the knowledge of how it was created. I'm sure the explanation is much more complex than my present understanding of it but I could reproduce the same effect again using the same principles and procedures.

Nature of Aura Field Distortion

The three aura energy fields which can be identified and measured using the dowsing technique are integrally locked together and respond as a total energy system. They are also integrally associated with the chakra system which appears as localized energy nodes distributed throughout areas of the physical body. The presence of the chakra system is well recognized by ancient Eastern philosophies. This auric energy system carries the spirit/soul intelligence which occupies the physical body and is a component of the energy system which leaves the body at the transformation we call death.

The auric energy system is composed of a higher order of energy outside our known and understood earth energy system. It characteristically does not conform to energy phenomenon presently identified by science because it exists as a higher order of energy. It can be mentally drawn and directed without regard to physical distance or earth time. Therefore, the healer, in directing auric healing energy, is limited only by his/her ability to mentally project intent and focus to initiate an energy transfer reflecting in a stimulation of the life force of the subject.

The process of rebalancing the aura fields often causes transient instability in the five senses relative to the severity of the field distortion. Often nausea or mild dizziness is experienced for a few minutes. It is important to be prepared to physically support the person or have them sit down until the sensation passes. Often there is a dramatic positive change in the person after the field is re-centered. The receptor of the channeled energy will begin to describe sharper sight and hearing as well as more balanced and expanded thinking.

Holes and depressions in the aura fields are the second most important conditions to search for. The physical body and the auric energy fields are mirror images of each other. What happens to one will cause a mirrored effect in the other. If a person, through an accident, damages the physical body, automatically the effect will be imprinted as a distortion, a hole, or depression in the auric energy field associated with the physical location of the injury. Severity of the effects will relate to the extent of the injury. Broken bones will produce focused holes in the aura in precisely the physical location of the break or damage in the case of other areas of the body.

The dowsing search of the aura fields lends itself well to locating and pin-pointing problem areas. Holes found in the aura field using the miniature L-rod will be larger in the outermost field (mental field) and will taper to a smaller area as it approaches the physical body, thus precisely locating the physical area of distress.

Holes and depressions in the aura fields are memory imprints of a life experience. Anomalies in the aura fields such as shifts, depressions or holes can be the imprint from physical injury or caused by an emotional trauma or outside influences commonly termed "spirit possession", a very complex phenomenon.

The Chakra System

From the writings of C.W. Leadbeater, the special atoms of vitality and life are stimulated from energy of a higher order (the will of God) which empowers it to attract six other atoms which arrange in definite form, thus making a sub-atomic structure of brilliance and extreme activity. This life force energy is represented as the hexagram or Star of David or ©ETHERIC TRANSPONDER (ET), in the physical three-dimensional plane.

The chakra system consists of a series of wheel-like spinning vortices which are in the inner aura, the etheric double. The seven major chakras are distributed throughout the physical body as shown in Figure 4 on page 17. They are an important part of the energetic system of the physical body and appear to serve as transformers connecting energy from the higher planes to the body. Each affects the physical body through the nervous system in their respective areas.

The vitality of the chakras can be measured with the client lying in a horizontal position. The trained dowser can then suspend a pendulum over the area of each chakra, noting its direction and speed of rotation and vitality by motion of the pendulum.

As healing work is performed with the client, spirit clearing, energy charging of the aura fields, etc. the chakras will respond by becoming more energetic. It has been stated in several references that the chakras may rotate either clockwise or counterclockwise but they should all be rotating in the same direction in the person being tested. The overall difference in the rotational direction of the chakras in different people most likely relates to a polarity difference between the dowser and the person being tested.

Each dowser must develop a personal scale of "normal" based on experience. We must remember that each of us has our own sensitivity level to this work. We are not calibrated as individuals to any standard except in a very general way as humans.

Spirit Possession and Its Complex Effects

For thousands of years, man has been aware that he is not alone in his existence, but coexisted with an invisible spirit world. References are made to this awareness in ancient tribal histories and various religious writings, including the Christian Bible.

In these references, unseen spirits are classified 'good spirits' and 'bad spirits'. The good spirits were described as angels in Christianity and were believed to give help and protection to the living. They, like the Christ figure, were believed to be representatives of God. They have been referred to as spirits of the Christ Light.

Bad or negative spirits were associated with the devil, Lucifer, and the demonic forces destructive to man. They are commonly categorized as dark forces. Common phrases referring to spirit possession are, 'the devil made me do it', 'what ever possessed you to do a thing like that', 'it has to be the work of the devil'. These statements have been used to explain away irrational acts or actions taken without logical explanation or in some cases without conscious memory of what occurred.

In an attempt to bring the subject of "spirit possession" into an acceptable concept of reality, my healing experience has been directed and focused on effects of forces and influences of spirit possession on the human entity. It is a very complex subject and becomes more complex as my research continues. Western science, philosophy, and logic cannot explain this aspect of reality and tends to ignore it. The natural law of opposites applies to the concept of good and evil as well as to all other aspects of the physical universe. We are naturally polarized with the God force; therefore, the negative forces are destructive to our life form.

I have come to realize that spirit possession is responsible for many human disorders, both physical and mental. Statistically, the effects of spirit possession are widespread in varying degrees among the population. Its effects of physical and mental dysfunction vary greatly from one person to the next. Continued research in performing aura clearings has revealed information on the nature, characteristics and dynamics of spirit possession on the human life form.

Spirit possession occurs in various forms and causes a

variety of distortions in the energy system of the living. Negative spirit possession interferes with mental processes resulting in distortions in the aura field which can be identified and measured. In many cases, the spirit does not possess the person by intent but has somehow become trapped in an energy field. These spirits are more than willing to leave given the energy and encouragement to do so. Possession can be self-generated, such as a person with obsession, multiple personality or fragmented personality, a 'frozen child'.

The variety of possession from external sources is extensive and, depending on their strength, type, and location, can produce a variety of damaging effects. Poorly regulated speech, animated movements, a staccato voice, high pitched whistles from the throat or low animal sounds such as growls or howls identify negative spirit possession and the attempt to control the body.

The presence of negative possession can be detected by measuring distortions in the aura fields. Their basic effects are found as aura field shifts off the central axis of the body and holes in the aura field in varying locations. The effectiveness of the negative energies depends to a great extent on where in the aura they are located. If the negative energy is located in the area of the head, it can initiate mental disturbances. If in the area of a chakra, physical problems associated with that particular chakra may occur as a result of the inactive chakra. In these cases, the effects appear as holes in the aura field.

A troublesome form of spirit possession is a situation where the spirit of a past living person interferes with the life of a living person. Occasionally, it is a relative to the living person. With some urging and a charge of energy, they will leave and move to the spirit realms where they can progress in their program.

Another possessing spirit type which I discovered in 1992 was that of an aborted baby. I have experienced many such cases associated with terminated pregnancies. However, all terminated pregnancies do not produce the spirit entrapment in the woman's aura field. This situation is the underlying cause of many female problems as it seriously affects the function of the solar plexus or spleen nerve centers and all organs and functions associated with them. This situation can be further complicated by guilt on the conscious level, a complex state at the subconscious level, and the trapped hormonal program residual of the pregnancy.

The presence of a human spirit trapped in the female energy field appears as a hole in the aura field associated with the solar plexus or spleen chakra. The chakra will often be shut down causing digestive problems. Curiously, the trapped human spirit will never respond to the term "negative spirit energy" when dowsing the nature of aura field anomalies.

Much of our susceptibility to poor physical and emotional health is caused by distortions and anomalies registered in the aura fields. The term "negative spirit energies" is a generic classification which encompasses a variety of types, all of which are damaging to our life energy system. In these terms their presence is viewed as undesirable because of their destructive mental and physical effects. Their presence is indicated by anomalies and distortions in the aura fields not relative to other causes. The mental or physical effect is evident through distortion and damage to our aura energy fields.

For research purposes I have chosen the all-encompassing term "negative spirit energies" in order to classify the phenomenon and its general overall destructive effect on our life form. These aspects could be considered part of our psychic makeup. However, the negative spirit energy and their effects to our life form can be removed through a mental process termed "spirit clearing" or "exorcism," a term used by the Christian church. Based, to some degree, on their effect and character I have given them broad classifications as follows:

1. **Earth-Bound Spirits**. These are spirits of past living people who remained in the earth plane after their death transition. This type identifies with human intellect and in rare cases is identified as a relative of the living person. In some instances their presence has been detected in buildings, often their former home.

2. **Non-Descripts**. These are typically the largest number of negative energies found in the aura energy system. Under this broad classification the presence of their larger numbers can cause a significant overall effect such as field distortion and holes in the field. These non-descript energies are shapeless and gray but possess a level of intelligence.

3. **Astrals**. The presence of energies responding to this classification are not commonly found. Where present their effects other than distortions of the aura has not been identified.

4. **Demonics**. The presence of energies under this classification is quite rare. However, this type is the most destructive with respect to our human life form. In varying degrees, they will take control of the body and will overpower the inborn spirit personality with their own negative personality. Their presence can cause physical distortion and chronic pain as well as mental instability.

There are many references to support the existence of spirit possession of the living. Recorded details can be found in

Catholic Church history and the Christian Bible as well as other religions of the world.

The spirit clearing procedure suggested was given to me by the highest order of Spirit/God and has been totally safe and successful.

Caution: I would not advise attempting spirit clearings without full spiritual protection and, if possible, proper instruction from an experienced person. This area of healing work is not to be treated lightly because it involves working outside the three-dimensional five sense physical aspects of life.

THE SPIRIT CLEARING PROCESS:

1. Request permission from the God Power to perform a spirit clearing of negative energies using the yes or no dowsing procedure. If the answer is no or indecisive, do not proceed further. Timing might be a factor and might change to a yes at a later time. It is important to request permission in advance before making further arrangements.

2. It is important to review the planned procedure with the client so that he/she understands what will take place. You must receive permission from the client to begin the clearing process. Make sure that the spirit clearing process does not conflict with his/her personal belief system or religion.

3. Having previously scanned the aura fields for holes, depressions and shifts, the next step is to dowse for the number of negative spirit energies present in the client's energy system. Be sure to record the information so that both you and the client can review it later. If desired, the types of negative energies may be identified based

on the list previously given. The procedure, though, does not require that you pinpoint the type of negative energy present.

4. Stand facing the person and repeat aloud the following statement of protection: "I cover myself with the White Light of Christ. Nothing but good can come to me, nothing but good can flow from me. I ask the God Power and my spirit guides to gently and safely remove the negative energies from this person's aura. Return the negative energies to their proper place in the spirit realm."

5. The negative energies should be removed through the crown chakra proceeding as follows: With the client standing (or sitting in a chair, if necessary), place one hand, palm open, fingers spread to access a source of energy, etheric field or random hot spot.

Place the other hand, palm down, fingers spread about 2 to 3 inches over the person's head. While slowly rotating the hand in a **clockwise** direction repeat the following statement: "I ask the negative spirit energies to please leave this body and return to the spirit realms where you belong. God will be your guide."

During this procedure, often there will be electric tingling or heat felt in the palm of the hand as a signal to quickly raise the hand vertically and away from the head. It is important to observe the client's stability and, if necessary, support him/her for a short time until they become stable; assuring the client's safety.

Dowse to find out the number of negative energies remaining so that you are aware of how the program is progressing. The strongest energies will typically be the last to leave the body. As you progressively remove negative energies and reach a point where the numbers no longer drop, you will likely need to extend your charging time with the etheric energy source to raise your energy as the remaining negative energies progressively increase in strength. As the facilitator, your energy level must always be higher than the negative energy level in order to release them from the client's energy field.

It is advisable to move through the clearing program at a steady pace to minimize their reaction to the process. Once started, the program should continue to completion. This is very important.

There may be expressions of suppressed emotions surfacing or the client may wish to describe experiences at each clearing procedure. He/she should be given time and encouraged to release trapped emotional energy if it is present. He/she might describe negative energies coming from various areas of their body. Typically, if there is a hole in the aura at the solar plexus or spleen chakra and it relates to a negative spirit energy, it will be the strongest and likely the last to leave in the clearing process.

It is possible that the procedure will trigger suppressed emotions or open up a past life experience. If this situation is recognized, the facilitator may bring the person back from the experience by placing a hand on his/her upper arm and softly assuring him/her that they are in the present now and all is well.

With a female client, if a hole in the aura at the solar plexus remains after the clearing, this may relate to the trapped human spirit of a terminated pregnancy or a trapped emotion relating to a past experience. It might also be a trapped human spirit resulting from a multiple pregnancy where one fetus did not survive.

When performing a spirit clearing of negative energies it is advisable to complete the work by energizing each of the seven major chakras. This can be accomplished by channeling energy and directing it in a clockwise rotation with the fingertips into each chakra. Six or seven rotational spins should suffice. Complete the charging by stroking the meridian flow clockwise facing the front then facing the back of the body. Four or five large clockwise sweeps should suffice after moving up and down energizing areas along the spine.

Healing Trapped Emotional Trauma Through Regression

Past life regression therapy is a very effective method of healing emotional distress caused by any number of life or past life traumas. As we travel through this earth life we all are exposed to painful emotional experiences which leave imprints of emotional trauma locked in our subconscious often without conscious memory. These emotions can drastically affect our life pattern and cause us serious pain and unhappiness. We can become emotionally overloaded without an effective way of self processing and releasing these painful emotions.

The conscious mind is oriented to the five sense input and processing of logic data in the three-dimensional world of reality. It is primarily ego driven to support and provide protection for the physical organism. It is quite limited and ill equipped to process major emotional trauma. In an attempt to rid itself of this painful burden it will often attempt to suppress the memory of the experience or erase it from the memory.

The conscious mind functions as a transformer on the earth plane absorbing data through the five senses to be synthesized into a physical reality which functions with reasonable predictability. Unpredicted occasions of a threatening nature place the conscious mind in a state of chaos and disorganization. Recovery from this state may never be complete without deep psychotherapy involving the subconscious levels of the mind.

Emotional trauma polarizes and saturates the psychic and suppresses or distorts reality and the personality. Trauma might occur at any age even before birth or in a past lifetime. Traumatic experiences at earlier ages produce the most serious effects.

Past life regression therapy is a very effective method of healing emotional distress caused by any number of life or past life traumas. Painful emotional experiences leave an imprint locked in our subconscious where it can be hidden from conscious memory. These locked emotions can drastically affect our life pattern and cause serious pain and unhappiness. We become emotionally overloaded without a way of self processing.

The subconscious mind is a storage vault of life experiences. Everything that ever happened to you is recorded in great detail. Where the emotional level is high enough, it can trigger flash-backs into the conscious mind, thus generating a repetition of the initiating experience. The information relived is often fragmented and unintelligible to the conscious mind which retains only a vague or fragmented memory of the incident. However, the stored emotion can initiate an overwhelming surge of emotions in the conscious mind without a conscious recollection of the cause. The emotional history of a person greatly affects the projected personality and can set the stage for undesirable mental conditions such as depression, anxiety attacks, etc. The conscious mind attempts to fill the gaps around these fragments of memory whether from a logical or rational source or not. The true facts of an emotional experience are always present in the subconscious memory and accessible through 'past life regression'.

To free our spirit from painful trapped emotions we must identify and neutralize the negative emotional energies that are stored in the subconscious part of the mind. This must be performed in a state of mind where the ego is not actively controlling or interfering with the program. When your inborn spirit is distorted by painful experiences, the ego (protector) takes control. The ego is ill equipped to deal with serious emotional problems. Its primary drive is for survival. In a state of complete relaxation the facilitator can guide the client to approach and enter a dimension termed the "alpha state". At this level the client gains access to the recorded historical data of their past lives including the present one. Using a chronological progressive procedure, it is like running a motion picture of the client's life backwards and forward allowing time for the client to view and experience each frame. When the client is reconnected to the past experience they have the ability and with brief instruction can analyze, process, and discharge the trapped emotions associated with the experience.

It is important to record the regression using a cassette tape recorder and 90 minute tapes. This may be reviewed at a later time with the client to reinforce their conscious level mind of the experience and how the trapped emotions were processed.

PROCEDURE:

Begin with the client lying down and covered with a light blanket to retain heat. In the alpha state, the pulse rate slows and the client may feel a chill. It is important that the client has used the rest room before starting the regression proceedure to prevent disruption of the program once it has begun. The body and mind are lowered into the alpha state by sweeping the energy field of the client with your hand. It is important that the client is assured that the facilitator will be present and in full control of their voyage into the past. It is a good practice to hold the client's hand to assure them of your presence.

When the alpha state is reached the client's breathing will slow and deepen and they will then become very relaxed. Ask the client to imagine him/herself with you in a vehicle described as a beautiful iridescent blue bubble. Occasionally, the client will have difficulty transposing their age to the year of the incident. It may be necessary to convert their age to the calendar year of that age. You can descend backward through the sequence of years saying "your age is... and the year is..." It is important to move slowly allowing the client adequate time to search and recall the occasions of the year and age. If there is a suppressed emotion, it will be identified by a quickening or deepening of the breathing rate, physical movement, facial contortions and frequently, a few tears. Encourage conversation describing the experience with names and other details of the experience and how the client is involved.

Assure the client that you are with them and all is well. Tell them that they are in charge and can return to the present at any time by opening their eyes. Ask them if they are ready to begin the journey in the blue bubble which can freely move through time and dimensions. Advise the client that, ' together we are now in the blue bubble and descending through a count down to zero'; this will allow him/her to go deeper into alpha, beginning the journey back in time. If communication with the client is lost, it implies that they have passed the alpha window and must be brought back to the alpha level to restore communication. Begin with the year/age just before their present age, asking that they search each year for painful experiences or other experiences which they would like to talk about. To help with their recall ask them to briefly describe their feelings about their mother and father, adoptive parents,

67

siblings or husband/wife, etc. Assure the client that they will have another opportunity to review the ages on the return trip.

As the facilitator, it is <u>very important</u> not to interject your personal thoughts or suggestions into the client's program. In effect, it will divert their mental focus to your program rather than theirs, leading to serious confusion. Again, it is important to let the client develop their own information and feelings based on their recall of the experience. What the client perceives to be reality in the state of regression may seem illogical to the facilitator. However, the facilitator must accept the reality of the situation as fact based on the experience of the client.

As you move the client back year by year it is important to progress slowly and periodically ask, "How is everything at age _____ or year _____." Sometimes this will open the psyche to recall and they will become focused on details of past life experience, some of which may be quite pleasant.

Although the client must be in contact and experiencing a past life experience to be able to release the emotions trapped in it, it is not necessary for them to experience the pain of the experience. Therefore, if they begin to express pain or strong emotional anxiety, they should immediately be instructed that they are having the experience but they are not feeling any pain. If several attempts to release them from the pain is unsuccessful, they should be taken out of the experience by moving them in age past the year of the experience. When they have been taken out of the experience there will be immediate signs of calming. The age at the time of the incident should be noted for future work. <u>The client should never be left in a state of pain or emotional panic</u>.

In some cases, the client will advise in advance that "something is coming up." This indicates the emotion of an experience has begun to surface often the year before the actual occurrence. This can prepare the facilitator for entering into an emotional experience which the client must be allowed to process.

If, through the regression procedure, the significant trapped emotional trauma was not released, you should try the following. Before beginning the regression procedure, measure the vitality of the seven major chakras by suspending a pendulum over the energy centers as the client is lying down. In comparison, you may find that one or two of the chakras has a slower and smaller rotation. Make a note of your findings and after the client has descended into the alpha state, direct him/her to search the affected chakra for the trauma that is causing it's suppression. Once the trauma is identified, follow the procedure for discharging trapped emotional trauma. This is a very effective method for accessing a serious trauma very directly.

It is not necessary to take a client through their entire life or past life experiences in a single session. However, they should be taken through the stage of measuring the aura fields and performing a spirit clearing if necessary before past life regression work is attempted. It is important to take these steps in proper order.

It is advisable not to extend the first regression beyond the client's point of conception in this life time or the experience of a highly emotional state with which the client might not be able to identify. In cases of complex and major emotional experiences it is advisable to take the client only as far as they are able to successfully process and release the emotions involved. There is a factor of psychic fatigue which should be recognized as limiting the client's ability to successfully process emotional energies trapped in various experiences.

Time is not a critical factor in performing past life

Life Span Emotional Imprint Experience Chart

Typical experiences associated with emotional trauma trapped in the subconscious

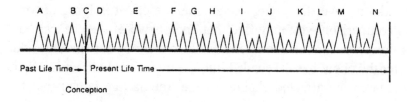

A	Past life trauma - Death experience
B	Past life trauma - Death experience
C	Conception
D	Gestation period - Imprinted emotional trauma of the mother
E	Birthing experience
F	Injury at age 2
G	Spanking experience - Physical abuse at age 3
H	Death of a parent - Grand parent age 5
I	Separation of a parent - Age 10
J	Remarriage of parents resulting in alienation of the child
K	Mental/Physical abuse - Drug and alcohol problems
L	Sexual abuse at any age
M	Unaccepted pregnancy - Abortion - Miscarriage (females)
N	Marriage relationship problems

Figure 13:

regression work. Therefore it is advisable to progress over several sessions where complex emotional experiences are present. Progressive regressions can be picked up at the age where the previous session terminated. After placing the client in the alpha state verbally that both of you are in an iridescent blue bubble and are going to travel directly to the age at which the previous session terminated. Then advise them that their age is now _____, and continue toward conception. To return, ask the client if they are ready to return or inform them that it is time to return to the present time. Using the image of the iridescent blue bubble again, count their age up to the present assuring them that all is well and they are relaxed and happy. It is important to pace the return allowing the client time to mentally register the ages as they are passed through, stopping if necessary to recall an emotional experience that may present itself.

Discharging Present and Past Life Emotions

Emotions trapped in the psyche can be viewed as high mountains, low mountains and rolling foot hills. See Figure 13. Searching through the past life history recorded in the subconscious mind you will most likely find all three levels. The high level emotional experiences will express themselves first, typically without much urging. The lower level of emotions, the lower mountains, each carry their stored memory of the experience that generated them. It is important to process these emotions through a simple process of forgiveness. Often at the lower levels of stored emotion the energy impact will be low enough so as to seem unimportant to the client. These weaker emotions are the rolling foot hills, which I view as typical day-to-day emotions which ebb and flow without deep or lasting effects on the psyche.

Once the client has made contact with a memory which begins to trigger the trapped emotions, it is important to allow

71

them time to adjust verbally to describe details of what is happening to them. It is helpful to ask brief questions such as, "Where are you? Who is with you? What is happening?"

Caution: The facilitator should never try to analyze or rationalize what the client is experiencing with them. Never imply blame of anyone to the client while in the regressed state.

It is extremely important that the facilitator remain neutral by offering affirmations such as, "yes, it's o.k., or I understand." This reassures the client that you are there and aware of what they are experiencing. They, in their mental processing, might express their innocence or guilt for the experience in young childish mannerisms.

Once the client is attached to or immersed in the experience as evident by their expression of emotion, the facilitator should instruct them with a firm voice, "Now, I want you to forgive yourself for the experience you had. I also want you to forgive any others involved in this experience." The client can do it aloud or silently but direct them to indicate when the forgiveness program is complete. You might have to repeat these instructions several times to capture their attention. A little coaxing may be required if the client is reluctant to forgive either themselves or persons identified as an offender.

You may convince them to forgive by telling them that, in order to free themselves, they must free the other person completely and without constraint. The forgiveness is part of the program of acceptance that the experience did actually happen and that it occurred in the past. Forgiveness is a symptom of release.

At this point, you may ask if the client is ready to go on. Occasionally, they will indicate that they require more time to complete their processing of the trapped emotions. Often, you will observe the emotional tension in the face begin to relax and the facial features will soften. This is accompanied by a slowing and deepening of the breathing or a silence. These are visual indications that the client has processed and discharged the trapped emotional energy which was attached to the experience. You may notice the client expressing a feeling of elation followed by a smile.

The above procedure must be carefully repeated each time the client enters an emotional experience. In some cases these emotional experiences occur in the womb during the gestation period or at the point of conception. Regardless of the point in this lifetime, the painful experience can be processed with the instruction to forgive.

To help the client establish focus and grounding it is well to have them repeat several affirmations before their return to the conscious level. For example: I am a child of my creator; I have incarnated on the earth plane to experience this place on my spiritual progression; I am an individual spirit being with God-given free will to manage my life for better or worse as I choose; I will fulfill my purpose in this life experience in a positive and constructive way which will comfort my soul and spirit.

Finally, it is important to slowly return the client to the present time assuring them that all is well and giving him/her the present time and location.

In Search of the Frozen Child

In this work it is quite common to find "the frozen child". There may be one or several fragments of the psyche dependent on the client's history. This situation occurs where the person experiences a trauma so intense that it fragments the psyche causing a part or parts to separate and react as though frozen in time at the age when the experience occurred. These mental conditions are described as a multiple personality or personality disorder.

The frozen child, when discovered and contacted, is frequently angry and expresses distrust because it identifies itself as having been abandoned. The distrust relationship with the parent psyche (the client) is what maintains the perpetual separation of the two. The parent psyche and the frozen child share the emotions of the trauma which initiated the fragmentation. The frozen child, under certain conditions of psychic recall can express its own personality and anger through the parent psyche. This might be termed an unstable personality in a child or adult by those who do not understand the principles behind the phenomenon. The frozen child appears to affect and distort the parent personality, causing unusual behavior such as spontaneous emotional outbursts even though the presence of the frozen child is hidden from the conscious mind.

Symptoms of the presence of a frozen child can be detected when reviewing the client's personal background and memory or lack of it. If they allude to the presence of a child, possibly with the client's own name, there is a good possibility of the presence of a frozen child. Spinning sensations, mental black outs or some other unusual activity described by the client may also allude to the presence of a frozen child.

Recovering the Frozen Child

When moving back in time, if the client experiences an emotional trauma which they cannot forgive, this is an indication of a frozen child. The facilitator must quickly advise the client to search for their child frozen in time. Often they will focus on themselves in the experience when taken to the age where the trauma occurred. At this point, the client should be instructed to talk to the child and plead with it to return to them. With continued instruction and encouragement by the facilitator, the client will be able to recover and integrate the frozen child into their psyche, thus discharging the emotions trapped in the experience.

The recovery and integration of a frozen child can take place in several ways. It may occur very quietly or it my be treated by the client as the recovery of an invisible baby. The client may talk to or pat it. Or it may integrate with a single jerk or convulsive movement of the client's body. After the integration, the client will experience a state of elation and well-being.

The client should be brought back to the present time and advised of the date, and their state of well-being as they arrive at their present age and open their eyes. It is a good idea to review the experience of the regression with them. After the recovery of a frozen child, the client should be given at least seven to ten days to emotionally stabilize before continuing the work to allow the conscious mind to process the work just performed. Upon completion of the work, the client can be invited to review his/her recording with the facilitator. This auditory review will reinforce the processing at the level of the conscious mind.

Case Histories

Mrs. S was a 35-year-old housewife with a husband and two young children. She had been experiencing mental problems for years and had tried various therapies without success. Her first statement was, "I feel like a stranger in my own family. I can't share love with my husband or my children."

She was aware of some of her background experiences but wasn't aware that she had a frozen child trapped at 9 years old. She was the oldest of four children. At 9 years of age, she had witnessed a murder committed by her father in the family home. The intense trauma of the experience had left a nine-year-old fragment of her psyche frozen in time twenty-six years in the past. Through several sessions of past life work she was able to recover her nine-year-old frozen child as well as another fragment which had suppressed her ability to express love. She is now a happy wife and mother.

Case History - Mrs. B. was an abused child who described horrible nightmares and the fear of a black shadow that followed her. It was suggested that the black shadow was a part of her, a frozen child. After several days, she called advising me that she now recognized it as a part of herself. We talked about the possibility of a life regression to search out the experiences causing these problems and process them, neutralizing the trapped emotions and remaining problems.

The regression was performed and among many experiences with trapped emotions we discovered an experience where she was cutting herself in a suicide attempt. This experience identified with the nightmares in her adult life and they abruptly stopped after she re-experienced the scene. As the regression progressed, we searched for a psychic fragment, a frozen child which we discovered as we regressed to age 14. It identified with a sexually-oriented experience. With coaching and encouragement she was able to communicate with the frozen child and within a few minutes it was recovered, reintegrating back into her psyche and freeing her inborn spirit to express itself in wonderful ways of spiritual understanding.

Recovering the Memory of a Lost Childhood

Many people have lost the memory of their childhood or in some instances their adult memory as a result of an experience such as war or other major trauma. They are often carrying emotions and self-imposed guilt associated with an experience identified with the lost memory. The unknown background history of a person can present a driving need to know the details of the past, especially when there are trapped emotions or fragmented flicks of memory from the past. Most often the recovery of the memory will satisfy the anxiety involved and discharge the trapped emotions. It might require a more focused approach to the age where the levels of emotion are found trapped within an experience.

Principles and Application of Thought Form Fields

Thought form fields are mental energy constructs existing outside the aspects of the physical three-dimensional plane. They are made up of a form of energy which can be mentally programmed and transmitted in a fashion similar to radio waves. These mental transmissions occur outside the physical dimensional system and therefore the energy flow does not conform to scientific principles of the three dimensions. Thought form energy can be transmitted mentally without respect to earth time and physical distances. The system can effect movement and changes in physical objects and materials and often is referred to as psycho-kinetics phenomenon, in

77

which a physical object can be made to move strictly through mental focus and intention.

Mentally generated thought forms can be transmitted over long distances through mental projection. A mental program generated with specific intent and intensely focused on another person can be effectively transmitted through the subconscious level of mind to the receiver and then to his/her conscious level through mental and/or physical effects. The positive aspects of the principle reflect positive effects to both persons involved. Transmissions as well as conscious level directed thought forms and thoughts conform to the absolute law of cause and effect. Healing remotely through photographs or other forms of focus is a well documented and effective method. This law does not differentiate between good and evil; therefore, it generates its own response. Caution: negative use of this ability will reflect back to the sender with equal or greater force than was used transmitting it.

Psychic Healing

Psychic or spirit healing are general terms used to describe processes involving manipulation of auric field energy to produce a mental/physical correction of a deficiency within the physical body. The aura energy fields are extremely important in providing life energy to support all body functions from the cellular level to the total concept of the human body. The process of generating or channeling aura energy to a client who is deficient in aura energy or has anomalies in their aura is all that is required to initiate a healing process. Right hand (clockwise) rotation of the hand used to direct energy will cause energy to flow to the client. Reversing the rotation to counter clockwise will cause energy to flow from the client to the healer. Short periods of reversing rotation (polarity) can be used to break up stubborn blockages in the energy system.

However, psychic healing work should always be completed by building the energy field with energy formed in a clockwise rotation. This procedure is described in Yoga healing techniques.

One of my earliest healing experiences was with a woman who had a left brain stroke three years prior that left her with a severe speech problem, a paralyzed right arm and difficulty on the right side of her body. While taking many readings of her aura fields, I found the field completely missing in an area on the left side of her head and a severely weakened aura on the right side of the body.

Her aura field was charged with channeled energy directing the energy into holes in the field. Within a few minutes time, she recovered full use of the paralyzed arm which she had been unable to use for three years. Progressively, over a three week period, and without further healing, her speech problem was completely corrected. The correction was permanent, with only a slight limp on the right side as evidence of the stroke.

Remote Healing

Remote healing is possible and can be accomplished on a mental level. This phenomena of human communication of intelligence over long distances is described in Yoga writing as well as the Huna philosophy of the Polynesians of the Pacific Islands (see references to Huna in the recommended reading list).

Much of my healing work is conducted remotely through photographs of the client and, in several emergencies, using only the name. My primary reason for working at a distance through photographs is to maintain a record of the case and its details as research data. An aura relating to the client will project from a photograph as long as the subject is alive. A photograph also serves to establish a conscious level contact with the client. This further strengthens the channel of communication over which the energy will travel and provides a flexible method of working with the energy system irrespective of physical distance.

The emanation of auric energy from the human body conforms to a holographic principle. Each cell radiates the full aura as does the whole body. A human blood spot, even if old and dried, will radiate the aura of that person as long as they are still alive on the earth plane.

It is interesting to note that people of the Amish religion and, in the early days of photography, the American Indians, didn't want their pictures taken because they believed the photographer was carrying away part of them.

There are many limitations when working through photographs in collecting detailed research data because of the two dimensional aspects of the photo. However, this problem has no effect in limiting the communications and transmission of intelligence and channeled healing energy to the client.

Time is unimportant in conducting remote healing. The transmission of the intelligent program of intent and its associated energy occurs instantaneously between the mind of the dowser and the client irrespective of physical distance.

There may be cases where it is advisable to establish a correlated time to perform the healing with the client. This can heighten the healing effect by allowing the client to be comfortable and mentally prepared to accept the healing energy transmission. The correlation of timing may also be important to allow the client to be in the presence of a friend or parent to provide comfort when the client begins to release emotions associated with his/her problem.

These requirements must be evaluated on an individual basis by the healer's suggestion or the client's request. The factor of timing is only effective at the conscious level of the client's mind and has no effect on the healing transmission. The healing process is automatic and does not rely on client participation. Ideally a trust relationship with the client should be established. It is important to review the healing process to ensure there are no conflicting religious constraints. If the client is uneasy, it is best not to proceed.

PROCEDURE:

1. Obtain a photograph of the client. The photograph acts as a mental focus for the dowser. It is preferred that the photograph show only the client. It is difficult to separate the auras of different people and animals projecting from a photograph. Typically with more than one person, or an animal in the photo you will be reading the one projecting the largest aura. A masking-off procedure can be used if necessary.

    A three quarter view of the subject is O.K. Photo dowsing follows a holographic principle. Therefore, every cell of a person's body showing in the photo will project the person's aura. The full aura can be read from any part of the person's body showing in the photo. The age or size of the photograph is not important. The aura field projected will be relative to that of the body at the present time.

2. It is <u>important</u> before proceeding to ask permission from Spirit/God. Use the dowsing rod to get a yes or no. A "no" means <u>STOP</u>. Try again later.

3. Using a stiff measuring rule placed against the photo,

record the point at which the small (six inch) dowsing L-rod turns parallel to the photo surface and crosswise to the rule. This reading will be the surface of the outer aura, the mental and emotional body projecting from the photo. These measurements cannot be compared between different dowsers because our sensitivity levels to the aura energy varies. Therefore, we must develop our own evaluation of the readings based on personal experience.

4.   Using the dowsing rod, held facing the photo, ask the question, "Are there negative energies present in this aura field?" You must have previously received spirit permission and have determined the L-rod movements which indicate "yes" and "no". My personal program is to the right for yes, and left for no. However, I am left handed so it might be reverse for you.

Most everyone has the presence of some 'negative energies' which detract or suppress the human aura field emanating from the body and photo surface. On the photo we are reading average aura emanations from the body.

A spirit clearing should be conducted following previously given instructions and visualizing the photo of the person. Working at this level of mind, there is no difference between conducting the clearing in person or through a photo.

5.   Charge the aura field with channeled energy immediately after the clearing to prevent return of some number of negative energies. After the aura energy stabilizes from its oscillations, (this should take 30 to 60 minutes) check the stable reading of the aura fields. It should stabilize at a much greater reading than originally measured. The field on the photo should be checked periodically and charged if necessary over a week or so. A sudden drop in

the field could indicate the return of negative energies or a repeated depletion of the field could indicate the person is being radiated by geopathic fields in his/her home or work place. (Refer to section on *Geopathic - Noxious Fields and Their Effects* for further instruction).

Case History - Missing Child

A thirteen year old girl ran away from home. The parents had searched all night for her without success. The frantic mother contacted me and I requested a photograph of the girl. I quickly developed contact with the girl, performed an aura clearing, and transmitted a mental message - *Call your mother - Call your mother*. Within two hours, I received a call from the mother advising that the girl had called asking her mother to pick her up. Further work with the girl and mother completely healed the problem between them.

Case History - Boy Missing for 9 Years

A friend and fellow worker had asked me if I could help him find his missing son. He related that his 15-year-old son was involved with drugs and alcohol and had suddenly disappeared 9 years ago. He gave me a small wallet size photo of the boy to work with. Scanning the photo, I found a very weak aura field. The registry of an aura on the photo indicated that he was alive. I performed a spirit clearing of negative energies from him. There were 185 present, the largest number I have ever encountered. I then continued to charge his aura with programmed energy for three days. The fourth day I received a message from the father that his son had contacted the family through his sister. He told her of his strange experience as a street person in Chicago. He described experiencing something resembling an epileptic seizure in which he recovered his memory of who he was and where he was from. After nine years he was reunited with his family and after a period of therapy became a responsible citizen.

Case History - Healing in Germany Through Photo in Pennsylvania

A woman in New York City sent me a photo of a young girl and asked if I could help her. There was no further information.

I checked the aura on the photo. It was very weak. I then checked for negative energies and with Spirit approval removed them. With several energy charges, the girl's aura responded and balanced as measured on the photo. Five days after I had received the photo, I received an excited call from New York. The woman had just received a call from Munich, Germany that the girl's severe depression problem had vanished and there would be no need for her to go through the planned electrical shock treatment. Several months later, I received a very nice letter from the girl in Germany and a gift which I prize highly.

Spirit Guides

To access the realms of our spiritual reality we must accept the concept of spirit contact as a possibility. As I began to have healing experiences that were totally unexplainable in any form of scientific logic I turned to the principles of the Spiritualist Church for answers. Through guidance from Spirit toward incredible healing experiences, I accepted the possibility of spirit help, and was able to bring into my reality the availability of spirit guides. Spirit guides assist and provide protection when exploring and discovering our connections to these mysterious realms. They are not permitted to violate our God given free will and therefore can only participate in the work by invitation.

There is much that we don't know or understand about the dimensions of being which are outside the physical plane of existence. Spirit Guides are highly evolved souls who volunteer to interface with humanity through visions, dreams, or waking inspiration. Most people do not actually "see" their guides but are aware of their presence. The insight they offer benefits us from their viewpoint which encompasses a wider range than we experience in physical. A spirit guide's hindsight from experience on the physical plane is an education beyond what one can learn in a single lifetime. Each guide has at least one particular area of expertise regarding physical earth plane existence, such as science or music. Most likely, the guide has had more than one lifetime honing that particular skill. Because of their high order of intelligence and ability to guide us and provide needed protection in spirit work, it is important to develop a trusting relationship with your available guides. Be certain that the spirit guide is of God, for your highest and best good, and part of the divine right order. Simply state that you will work with none other than the aforementioned.

Over a period of years, I have identified the presence of four spirit guides in my life. They are available at all times providing instruction in healing work and protection against the ever present destructive forces in the physical as well as spiritual realms. My spirit guides contact me at the proper time for my progression into uncharted dimensions of spiritual reality.

The first to initiate contact was Agawatha. With my inner vision, she appeared as a tall, stately American Indian woman. She projects the essence of a nurturing mother of human life. She is ever present in guiding spiritual healing work, the essence of universal motherhood.

The second spirit guide I found was Dr. Walter Russell who, through his works, was an enlightened genius while on the earth plane. It was through a very unusual experience that I was introduced to Walter. My wife and I, through a personal invitation, visited Swannanoa, a beautiful marble palace located on top of the Blue Ridge Mountains near Waynesboro, Virginia. Swannanoa was the home of Walter and his wife, Lao. Walter died in 1963 and Lao in 1993.

When we arrived, we were met by Lao and given a personal tour of the palace where Walter's art and sculpture were displayed. Lao invited us to her private quarters where the subject of discussion focused on spirituality, psychic phenomenon and the seriousness of world affairs, atomic weapons and the Cold War with Russia. My wife and I were both awestruck by the experiences we had that day.

Swannanoa has since become The University of Science and Philosophy. Tours or information on Dr. Russell's books can be obtained by calling (800) 882-LOVE or by mail: P.O. Box 520, Waynesboro, VA 22980.

I later discovered I could communicate with Walter through my small dowsing L-rod. Our working relationship, always on a scientific level, grew stronger with time. Several years ago, through communication with Walter, I was given instructions to assemble a crystal wand which develops a corona energy glow when psychically charged. This instrument has been an extremely important tool in my psychic research; however, it defies scientific explanation.

After a number of rather spectacular healing experiences, I began to wonder how these things happen. Within a short time, Walter spoke to me in the middle of the night and gave me a lecture much like a college professor. The subject was resonance. He spoke about the many forms of energy resonance including auric energy resonance called "prana" by the Eastern Yogis. He advised that mental psychic energy focused by specific intent and brought into a state of resonance was the key to transferring auric energy from one person to another to initiate healing. Apparently, Walter is taking advantage of my mental quiet time to communicate at that late hour.

Another night time lecture came through after I had been trying to rationalize the compression of earth time in performing past life regression work. Walter stated, "The universe is a gigantic clock with many parts. Your earth time is established on the cyclic movement of the sun and moon. When you move out of the three-dimensional earth time, time itself doesn't exist."

Over the past year Walter has been communicating through channeling with a close friend. The communication is very technical and involves interesting terminology and word usage.

Fong is an ancient Chinese philosopher who communicated as a guide several years ago. Fong doesn't become involved until after experiences happen. He then summarizes the event with an overall philosophical explanation. William James is the most recent spirit guide to reveal himself in my work. I suspect his presence indicates the evolving of a new phase of metaphysical work.

Quartz Crystals: Their Effects in Healing Work

Quartz is a common material in the earth's geological structure and is present in a variety of forms based on its content of minerals and other elements. Quartz crystals are a special geological formation with very unusual properties. The ancient Yogi's describe them as a primitive life form because of their response to various forms of energy stimulation. The best known of these responses is presently termed "pizo electric effect". Quartz crystals can be electrically pulsed and will respond at a fixed frequency based on their physical mass. This principle is used in radio transmitters to set their transmitting frequency. Quartz crystals also respond to a broad spectrum of energies including the human aura field.

Quartz crystals which are of special interest to the healer can be found in a number of places in the US and Canada and many places throughout the world. One of the best known sources of quality quartz crystals is in Arkansas. There are a number of commercial mining companies operating in the areas of Hot Springs and Mt. Ide.

Crystals of interest to healing work are the single terminated crystal with six sides (a hexagram) and a point on one end. The other end will have a rough surface where it has been removed from the crystal bed where it was attached.

Quartz crystals have individual characteristics based on many factors of their growth which occurred over thousands of years of earth's evolution. However, all single terminated crystals characteristically conduct energy flow in one direction similar to a crystal laser instrument. The charging flow direction will be energy flowing in through the six-side surfaces and fracture end and out through the pointed end. They can be used individually to direct energy into specific areas of a client's body which has a deficiency of energy (holes in the aura field.)

A simple crystal wand can be quite effective in directing energy. See Figure 14.

The crystal wands shown can be charged to a much higher energy level than a crystal used alone. Because of its tick-tock pulsing design using a wire coil arrangement, design reference B can be charged to extremely high energy levels. The shaft is thin wall brass tubing 3/8" diameter by 12" long which can easily be purchased from a hobby shop. The crystal fitted into

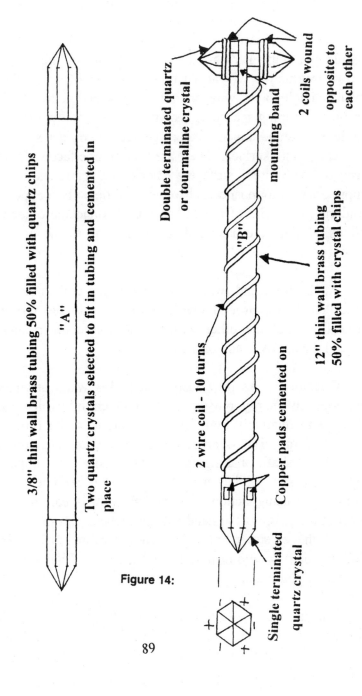

3/8" thin wall brass tubing 50% filled with quartz chips

"A"

Two quartz crystals selected to fit in tubing and cemented in place

Double terminated quartz or tourmaline crystal

2 coils wound opposite to each other

mounting band

"B"

2 wire coil - 10 turns

Copper pads cemented on

12" thin wall brass tubing 50% filled with crystal chips

Single terminated quartz crystal

Figure 14:

89

the discharge end should have a reasonably centered point (all flat surfaces on the point nearly equal to provide better focus and intensity of emitted energy. A double terminated crystal should be mounted crosswise at the back for rod reference B. A rod of tourmaline will also work. The coil of small diameter insulated telephone wire should be wrapped 8 to 10 times around the tubing spaced as shown. The two coil wires are then soldered to small copper pads cemented one on a + surface and the other on a - surface. There are three + side facets alternately arranged with three - surfaces. Choose one + and one - surface approximately opposite each other to mount the copper pads, soldering one wire of the coil to the plus and the other to the minus. Mount the pads and fasten the coil to the tube using epoxy cement.

At the back end, wind one wire of the coil three or four times clockwise around one end of the double terminated crystal. Wind the other wire of the coil counter-clockwise around the opposite end of the crystal.

Operation: As previously noted, this wand arrangement provides an energy pulsing (tick-tock) circuit which can be charged to relatively high levels of output in the form of an energy beam. The wand is charged by wrapping your hand around the shaft, shaking the crystals inside the copper tube lightly to assist the charging. As the crystals become energized from the pulsing action, the energy emitted can be felt by placing the palm of the hand several inches from the discharge end of the crystal point. The energy beam can be felt as tingling, heat or cold or may be felt like a wind blowing on the surface of your hand.

Wands are typically used to direct high levels of concentrated energy into holes in the aura field and are especially useful in energizing damaged disc areas of the back and damage to the nervous system where chronic pain is felt.

Male/Female Sexuality

Human sexuality is often the focus of emotional disturbances found in spirit healing and past life work. Sexuality is a primary part of our male/female programming in the earth plane and presents a number of interesting aspects to human life. Both sexes can experience emotional damage in varying degrees by sexually-oriented experiences which are viewed as violations of the ego self. These experiences can produce different effects such as depression, guilt, low self esteem, and many others.

Monitoring female aura fields has revealed a number of interesting aspects to the relationship between the energy system and certain physical female experiences. During ovulation, a hole in the aura will identify the active ovary. Throughout the period of pregnancy the aura energy fields will display an unusually large bulge in the lower abdominal area and the overall aura surrounding the body will be expanded to a significant degree. See Figure 15.

Women who have terminated a pregnancy through miscarriage or abortion will sometimes (but not always) display a hole in the aura fields in the area of the solar plexus nerve center (near the navel). A hole in the aura on the back at the same level implies that the solar plexus chakra is shut down. This might also happen to the spleen chakra which is lower in the abdominal area. This situation can be initiated by other conditions but if other possibilities such as negative energy possession have been eliminated, and if the hole in the aura at the solar plexus or spleen chakra persists it implies that, most likely, there is the presence of a trapped spirit associated with the fetus. There appears to be a short time period within which the spirit has freedom to come and go before permanent assignment to physical occurs. Therefore there are many variables between individuals in these experiences.

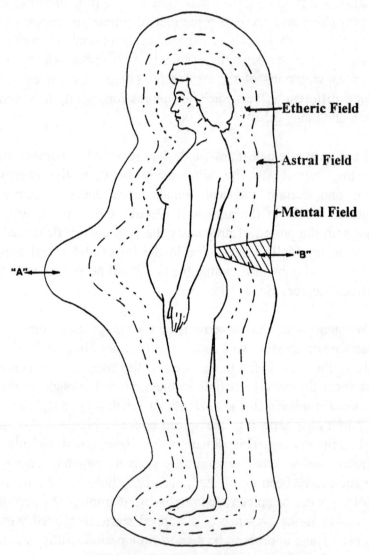

REF. "A": Enlarged aura of a female during pregnancy
REF. "B": Hole in Aura - Indicating lower back problem

Figure 15:

The trapped spirit causing the hole in the aura can be freed to the spirit realms by the person's willingness to let it go, and a charge of auric field energy to facilitate the release. The release procedure is conducted on a very high spiritual level, is very safe, simple, effective and permanent.

A terminated pregnancy through miscarriage or abortion, and frequently the circumstances associated with pregnancy, can initiate severe and lasting emotional trauma. Again, the severity of the emotions generated are variable based on the nature of the experience and the person's ability to cope with it. Termination of a pregnancy can leave the remainder of the incomplete hormonal program trapped in the woman's aura field. This situation can initiate long term emotional and physical health problems. The situation can be further complicated by self-blame, guilt on the conscious and spiritual level and a state of serious mental confusion. These states can also be initiated by childhood abuse, sexual molestation and rape.

Trapped baby spirits resulting from dual or multiple fertilization are a possibility. In some cases, as occasionally seen through a sonogram, more than one fetus is found present and an incomplete development occurs. It is possible that the spirit or spirits of the incomplete fetus will remain trapped in the woman's energy field. In experiencing this type of program, I use the same procedure for that of a terminated pregnancy.

There are effective ways of working through these life crippling experiences. However, these procedures require more than can be written and require closely supervised instruction for the student performing this work. Therefore, detailed description will be discussed in greater detail during workshop programs focused on these areas.

Positive Spiritual Factor

Perfect health as taught by Yoga philosophy emphasizes the importance of performing exercises which will increase the supply of Prana (auric energy). This involves special deep breathing exercises, eating highly energized foods and fluids and performing other psychic exercises to raise the aura energy and stimulate physical body functions and healing for those not in perfect health. The source of our mental, physical and spiritual health comes from within and not from outside ourselves.

The Duality of Our Lives

We live in many levels or planes of existence. Presently we view ourselves as physical beings having a body of substance. From this vantage point we begin to realize that the physical body is made up of substances of earth aided by a conglomerate of compatible micro organisms. We also discovered that we live in a physical strata which expands in both directions based on dimensional size, the micro and macro perspective. As our technology grows we discover we can see things progressively smaller and also larger than our familiar surroundings. The limits of dimensional reality are unknown. As a spirit we are also part of myriad dimensions of a spiritual reality. Therefore, in this vast concept of reality, we have an opportunity to participate in the cosmic master plan.

Personal Trauma of the Author

When World War II began to involve the USA, I was in high school and not realizing it until I began my healing research, I was being traumatized by listening to Hitler's powerful emotional speeches threatening to rule the world, broadcast to all the children in the auditorium. I was drafted into the army in my 19th year and had many traumatizing experiences as did many other men and women during the war time.

Upon returning home from the war there was little reference to it back in civilian life and I was able to suppress the memories and emotions of it for forty years until the death of my wife in 1991. The emotional experience of her death opened the door to emotions of war which I had guarded so well and now I was overwhelmed with a flood of emotions all triggering recall of experiences that had generated them. With time I was able to gain control with the help of a psychotherapist to re-experience these traumas and discharge their emotions through forgiveness.

I have always had a strong curiosity about who we really are, why we are here and what makes us tick. The focus of my curiosity became more intense after working as a medical technician with war casualties who had experienced states of mental collapse caused by war trauma. It wasn't until I became a water dowser or diviner, and much later a healer using the dowsing techniques, that I began to understand the workings of the human mind and the keys to entering the mental system and connecting mental and emotional disturbances as well as physical problems originating from a mental source.

I did much soul searching before I decided to write this book to reveal the experiences I had and what I had learned in communicating with my spirit guides. I also gained a great deal of information from clients and other people who would tell me of their experiences knowing that I would understand what they were describing and that it was safe to discuss these experiences with me.

I was well aware that some would describe me as "off the

wall," "way out there", etc. Some of these people were long time friends and even relatives. My 95-year-old mother-in-law, Marie, always understood what I was experiencing because she was communicating and seeing spirit people which she could describe in detail, over the last eight years. She is looking forward to her spiritual passing as a wonderful event. I am also looking forward to mine as an event to be celebrated and not mourned. A new experience.

Past Life and Channeled Experiences

My first psychic experience was at a lecture program in Chicago about 14 years ago. The program director, after a few hand motions, directed us to look at our feet and to notice what type of shoes we were wearing. Much to my surprise when I looked down I was wearing sandals with metal buttons at the strap crossings. I looked at my clothing. I was wearing a white linen tunic. Then I focused on what I was doing and I found myself in a Byzantine cemetery standing at the edge of a path. I was meeting the graveyard body bearers and instructing them as to which crypts to deliver the bodies, and recording the information on parchment.

It was a fascinating experience; the details were very logical based on the time period in history and very deeply imprinted in my conscious mind as a real happening.

The second experience was rather short and occurred approximately two years after the first. Working with a friend, I saw a dark skinned Eastern Indian woman before me. She was dressed in light blue veils with a darker blue veil over her head. She began to move and held out her hand beckoning me to come with her. She took me to an ornate Buddhist temple. We entered and there were a number of small stocky Buddhist monks sitting in the area. There were no auditory sounds of conversation but there was a mental communication in which they were offering to teach me their secret forms and techniques of spiritual healing. I never had any further contact with them, but in my healing research much of what I do is orchestrated by the intuitive rather than the conscious mind.

Working with another friend I had an out-of-body experience. I found myself without a physical body, moving through space high above a vast body of water and then over land. Rushing wind caused waves in large fields of grain. I then focused and descended to a cottage with a thatched roof that appeared to be somewhere in England. Surrounding the cottage was the typical English garden with colorful hollyhocks. I have always had an affinity for hollyhocks but never knew why. I was suddenly inside the cottage where a middle aged woman was tending to her duties. There was fire burning in the hearth and I felt a close and loving relationship to the woman although I couldn't identify how we were related.

Suddenly, the scene changed and I could hear the crashing of the surf against the cliff. In the distance the remains of an ancient stone castle and nearby was a small Celtic stone church and cemetery. I focused on a particular weathered stone in the cemetery. The name was MacIlvein, my Scottish grandmother's name in this lifetime.

The latest experience while working with another friend was quite interesting and was more oriented toward channeling. The technique used classical music with accelerated rhythmic changes. I saw wild geese flying gracefully in slow motion, then a ballerina dancing in slow motion. My body began to shake from head to foot and I advised my friend not to be alarmed, that I was in the process of leaving my body. In this state I began making predictions and statements which seemed to be oriented to the human race as a whole rather than a localized experience. I could hear my voice talking but my conscious mind didn't seem to be generating the information. It was me speaking but it was someone else's information. I re-entered my body, again going through jerks and jolts upon re-entry, and became consciously alert.

Highlights of the channeling are as follows:

"We are part of a cosmic order that transcends time and space. We are composites of many things suspended between the micro and macro levels of reality. We also live on other planes of existence simultaneously with our earth life. To gain understanding of these lives, we must project ourselves to be whole and perfect. We must understand who we are. We are not our bodies - we are Spirit."

My spirit guide, Walter Russell, says that we are projected through resonance which projects on all levels. The universe is in resonance; all parts vibrating in resonance. We project energy through resonance, mental resonance. We can project intelligence through resonance and can move from one plane of existence to another. Communication at the level of pure entrained resonance surpasses all other forms of communication.

There are many earth changes taking place. Changes like the earth has never experienced before. Find freedom without limitation by realizing that we are not limited by the earth plane. Energies are projected through mental processes. Project a positive mental thought and it will take place. It will take but a short time to alter the state of the earth plane and the people of the earth plane if we project positive thoughts. Energy will move from mind to mind as an energy wave of positive information, projecting, love, health and well being among people of the earth plane.

I bring forth from Spirit this information that you might use it to bring yourself and others into closer reunion with our ultimate source and those of the spiritual planes which support and comfort us in our journey through our earth life to our destiny in spirit.

Recommended Reading

Achterberg, Jean, *Imagery in Healing: Shamanism and Modern Medicine*: Shambhala, Boston.

Beasley, Victor R., Ph.D, *Your Electro-Vibratory Body*: University of the Trees Press, California.

Berkeley Holistic Health Center, *The Holistic Health Handbook*: AND/OR Press, California.

Binder, Betty, *Past Life Regression Guidebook - How Our Past Lives Influence Us Now*: Reincarnation Books/Tapes, California.

Bird, Christopher, *The Divining Hand*: E.P. Dutton, New York.

Bowles, Norma and Hynds, Fran, *Psi Search*: Harper & Row, San Francisco.

Brennan, Barbara Ann, *Hands of Light*: Bantam, New York.

Cagan, Andrea, *Awakening the Healer Within*: Fireside Book - Simon & Schuster, New York.

Carlson, Richard, Ph.D. (ed.) and Shield, Benjamin (ed), *Healers on Healing*: Jeremy P. Tarcher, Inc., Los Angeles.

Cerutti, Edwina, *Mystic with the Healing Hands - The Life Story of Olga Worrall*: Harper & Row, New York.

Condron, Barbara, D.M., B.J. (ed), *Total Recall - An Introduction to Past Life & Health Readings*: SOM Publishing, Missouri.

Fortune, Dion, *Psychic Self Defense*: Samuel Weiser, Inc, Maine.

Goldberg, Dr., Bruce, *Past Lives, Future Lives:* Ballantine Books, New York.

Hardy, Dean and Mary, *Pyramid Energy - The Philosophy of God, The Science of Man*: Delta-K Pyramid Products of America, Michigan.

Kaslof, Leslie, J., *Wholistic Dimensions in Healing, A Resourse Guide*: A Dolphin Book, Doubleday & Company, Inc., New York.

Leadbeater, C.W., *Man, Visible and Invisible*: A Quest Book, Theosophical Society Publishing, Illinois.

Long, Max Freedom, *The Huna Code in Religions*: DeVorss & Co., California.

Long, Max Freedom, *Psychometric Analysis*: DeVorss & Co., California.

Markides, Kyriacos, C., *Fire in the Heart - Healers, Sages and Mystics*: ARKANA, Penguin Books, New York.

Maurey, Eugene, *Exorcism - How to Clear at a Distance a Spirit Possessed Person*: Whitford Press, Pennsylvania.

Monahan, Evelyn M., *The Miracle of Metaphysical Healing*: Parker Publishing Company, Inc., New York.

Norman, Ruth, and Spaegel, Charles, *Principles & Practice of Past Life Therapy*: Unarius Educational Foundation, California.

Prophet, Elizabeth Clare, *Djwal Kul Intermediate Studies of the Human Aura*: Summit University Press, Los Angeles.

Ramacharaka, Yogi, *The Life Beyond Death*: The Yogi Publication Society, Chicago.
Ramacharaka, Yogi, *Fourteen Lessons in Yogi Philosophy and Oriental Occultism*: The Yogi Publication Society, Chicago.

Ramacharaka, Yogi, *The Science of Psychic Healing*: L.N. Fowler & Co, Ltd., London.

Ross, T. Edward, and Wright, Richard D., *The Divining Mind - A Guide to Dowsing and Self-Awareness*: Destiny Books, Vermont.

Scott, Mary, *Kundalini in the Physical World*: ARKANA, Penguin Books, New York.

Weiss, Brian L., *Through Time into Healing*: Simon & Schuster, New York.

About the Author

Tom Milliren is a retired engineer from the General Electric Corporation in Erie, Pennsylvania. He is a lifetime member of the American Society of Dowsers located in Danville, Vermont where he is a frequent teacher and lecturer on the many aspects of dowsing. He also lectures around the country on healing, aura clearing, and regression work. Currently, he lives in Erie, Pennsylvania with his cat, Lucky.